The impact of guns on women's lives

Amnesty International (AI) is an independent worldwide movement of people who campaign for internationally recognized human rights to be respected and protected. It has more than 1.8 million members and supporters in over 150 countries and territories.

www.amnesty.org

The **International Action Network on Small Arms** (IANSA) is the global movement against gun violence – a network of more than 500 civil society organizations active in 100 countries. Members work to reduce the availability and misuse of small arms and light weapons through advocacy and campaigning, research, information, awareness raising and victim support.

Email: contact@iansa.org, www.iansa.org

Oxfam International is a rights-based confederation of affiliated organizations working in more than 100 countries to find lasting solutions to poverty and injustice. Oxfam affiliates are working together with others to build a global movement of citizens campaigning for economic and social rights. Oxfam International believes that economic growth must be balanced with social equity to achieve a just and sustainable world: Oxfam America, Oxfam-in-Belgium, Oxfam Canada, Oxfam Community Aid Abroad (Australia), Oxfam Germany, Oxfam Great Britain, Oxfam Hong Kong, Intermón Oxfam (Spain), Oxfam Ireland, Novib Oxfam Netherlands, Oxfam New Zealand, and Oxfam Québec.

www.oxfam.org

i

First published by Amnesty International, the International Action Network on Small Arms (IANSA) and Oxfam International in 2005.

Copies of this report are available to download at
www.controlarms.org

ISBN 0-86210-368-1
AI Index: ACT 30/001/2005
Original language: English

Printed by:
The Alden Press
Osney Mead, Oxford
United Kingdom

The impact of guns on women's lives is published by:

Amnesty International
International Secretariat
Peter Benenson House
1 Easton Street
London WC1X 0DW
United Kingdom
www.amnesty.org

Oxfam International
Oxfam International Secretariat
Suite 20, 266 Banbury Road
Oxford OX2 7DL
United Kingdom
www.oxfam.org

International Action Network on Small Arms
(IANSA)
56-64 Leonard Street
London EC2A 4JX
United Kingdom
www.iansa.org

Contents

Chapter 1
Introduction

Sandra Stasenka holds a photo of her son Alex, a victim of gun violence, during a rally for additional gun control regulations. The rally on Capitol Hill, Washington DC, USA, was sponsored by Americans Against Gun Violence.

1: Introduction

There are estimated to be nearly 650 million small arms in the world today. Nearly 60 per cent of them are in the hands of private individuals[4] – most of them men. And the vast majority of those who make, sell, buy, own, use or misuse small arms are men. What does this mean for the world's women and girls?

This report looks at the impact on women of guns in the home, in communities and during and after conflict. In each of these contexts, it looks at violence committed with guns against women, the role women play in gun use, and the campaigns women are spearheading against gun violence.

Large numbers of women and girls suffer directly and indirectly from armed violence. Women are particularly at risk of certain crimes because of their gender – crimes such as violence in the home and rape.[5] And although available data supports the widespread assumption that most direct casualties of gun violence are men, particularly young men,[6] women suffer disproportionately from firearms violence, given that they are almost never the buyers, owners or users of such weapons.

Guns affect women's lives when they are not directly in the firing line. Women become the main breadwinners and primary carers when male relatives are killed, injured or disabled by gun violence. Women are displaced and forced to flee their homes for an uncertain future. Displaced women often face starvation and disease as they struggle to fend for their families. And women, like men, are caught in the crossfire, both in times of war and of peace.

Violence against women, whether committed with boots or fists or weapons, is rooted in pervasive discrimination which denies women equality with men.[7] It occurs in a variety of contexts and cuts across borders, religions and class. This is not because violence against women is natural or inevitable, but because it has been condoned and tolerated as part of historical or cultural practices for so long. Violence against women in the family and community, and violence against women as a result of state repression or armed conflict, are part of the same continuum: much of the violence that is targeted against women in militarized societies and during armed conflict is an extreme manifestation of the discrimination and abuse that women face in peacetime. Whatever the context or immediate cause of the violence, the presence of guns invariably has the same effect: more guns mean more danger for women.

Violence against women persists in every country and in all sectors of society. When such violence involves the use of weapons specifically designed to cause injury and death and which can fire bullets at high speed from a distance, sometimes at a rate of several bullets per second, then the risk to women's lives increases dramatically.

Women, men and guns

The relationship between women and guns is a complex one. Women are not only killed and injured by the use of weapons, they also play other roles – sometimes as perpetrators of armed violence, sometimes encouraging the use of guns, and sometimes as activists for change.

Women in many countries have become powerful forces for peace and human rights in their communities. This report includes the experiences of women who have been affected by gun violence and have decided to do something about it by calling for tougher arms controls, for safer communities, and for respect for women's human rights. Their campaigns are working to rid not only their own lives, but also those of their families and communities of the ravages of gun violence.

However, women's attitudes can sometimes contribute to the powerful cultural conditioning that equates masculinity with owning and using a gun, and regards gun abuse by men as acceptable. Women sometimes overtly encourage their men to fight, and, more subtly, support the attitudes and stereotypes promoting gun culture. Women and girls also actively participate in many of the world's conflicts, either willingly, through coercion, economic pressure, or because they have been abducted and forced to serve. For some women and girls in armed groups having a gun is seen as a way of protecting themselves and acquiring greater status. However, this is frequently illusory; and many girl and women combatants continue to be abused and are forced to commit abuses themselves.

The perception that a gun provides some measure of protection can be found in many different social contexts and is not confined to situations of armed conflict. Many men carry guns as part of their perceived and constructed role as "protectors" of women; the argument used by gun lobbyists is that they need guns to protect their families from armed intruders or attackers. But the reality of gun ownership and use is very different. Thousands of men in different countries are becoming actively involved in arms control campaigns that try to achieve greater security and safety for everyone and are also joining campaigns to stop violence against women. Some men

© Viva Rio

A poster from the Brazilian non-governmental organization Viva Rio, which launched a campaign with women's organizations under the slogan *Arma, Não! Ela ou Eu* (Choose gun-free! It's your gun or me) urging women to put pressure on their partners to hand in their guns.

are working alongside women specifically to challenge existing cultures of masculinity and the presumption that violence, including sexual violence, against women, is "normal" male behaviour.

Campaigns like the White Ribbon campaign, started by men in Canada to challenge men's silent complicity in violence against women, have gained support from men in Costa Rica, Denmark, Mexico, Namibia and South Africa, among other places. At another level, male former combatants and former gang members are among the people who can act most powerfully for change in challenging the links between violent expressions of masculinity and the gun culture.

Campaigning for change

This report provides an overview of where two major international campaigns intersect: **Control Arms** – organized by Amnesty International (AI), the International Action Network on Small Arms (IANSA) and Oxfam International – and AI's **Stop Violence Against Women** campaign. There is a growing acknowledgement that issues of gender need to be fully integrated into international work to stop the proliferation and misuse of small arms and that the specifics of armed violence have often been overlooked in some campaigns to address violence against women. More detailed analyses of many of these issues can be found in the reports published as part of the Control Arms and Stop Violence Against Women campaigns.

Chapters 2 to 6 describe how guns affect women in the home, in their interaction with law enforcers, in communities, and in and after conflict. These chapters end with brief action points outlining the most important measures that need to be taken to tackle violence against women and the proliferation and misuse of guns in these different situations. **Chapter 7** sets out the international legal framework that informs and underpins the campaigns to Stop Violence Against Women and Control Arms. The existing standards on violence against women need to be implemented properly, and new legal standards are required to curb the proliferation of guns. But legal recommendations are not the primary purpose of this report.

Chapter 8 looks at what we can do to stop the abuses highlighted. As well as lobbying for better laws and better implementation of existing laws, campaigners against violence against women and gun proliferation need to work to change attitudes. This is because new national and international laws, although essential, are not enough. Looking at how the myths about men, women, and guns

Marchers demonstrating in Cape Town, South Africa, about violence against women and children, November 2001.

are constructed can reveal new ways to break the cycles of violence which threaten to brutalize succeeding generations in so many societies around the world. We hope the varied experiences outlined in this report of how women and men around the world are campaigning to change hearts and minds will motivate you to join with them and do the same.

Stop Violence Against Women Campaign

AI's *Stop Violence Against Women* Campaign, launched in March 2004, shows that all women have the right to be free from violence.

Violence against women is universal, but it is not inevitable.

AI's campaign is designed to mobilize both men and women in organizing to counter violence, and to use the power and persuasion of the human rights framework in the efforts to stop violence against women. It calls on everybody – the state, the community and individuals – to acknowledge their responsibility to take action to stop this worldwide human rights scandal.

It's in our hands to stop it. We can end violence against women and we will end it with your support.

Control Arms Campaign **control arms**

The Control Arms Campaign launched in October 2003 by AI, IANSA and Oxfam International has supporters in over 100 countries. Using the Million Faces petition and a range of other activities, Control Arms campaigners are calling on governments to severely restrict arms in ways consistent with their international legal obligations and to introduce comprehensive arms control measures at all levels, from the suppliers to the users.

At the global level, governments should establish an international Arms Trade Treaty that would oblige governments not to transfer arms internationally if they are likely to be used to commit serious violations of human rights and war crimes.[8]

At the community and national level, the campaign is calling for measures to improve safety and the scope of non-armed security by enacting strict laws and procedures to control small arms; reducing the quantity of surplus and illegal arms in circulation; and improving the accountability and training of law enforcers and armed forces through work based on respect for international human rights and humanitarian law and standards. Campaigners are calling for more effective civic education about community safety to counter cultures of violence, including the destructive link between arms and conventional notions of masculinity.

Chapter 2

Armed violence against women in the home

© AP Photo/Kamenko Pajic

Main: Participants hold up a Columbine banner at the Million Mom March, 14 May 2000, Washington DC, USA. In April 1999, two students shot and killed 12 schoolmates and a teacher and wounded 23 other people at the Columbine High School in Colorado, USA.

Colorado
MILLION MOM MARCH

WHY do you need more than 1 GUN per month?? Stop the

The 2ⁿᵈ AMEND OUR FOREFATHERS DID NOT MEAN AUTO- ASSAU MATIC WEAPON

freedom from gun trauma

WE'RE LOOKING FOR A FEW GOOD MOMS MOBILIZE FOR COMMON SENSE GUN LAWS

Inset: Donna Dees-Thomases, a mother who came up with the idea for the Million Mom March, holds a poster for the gun control event.

2: Armed violence against women in the home

Violence against women in the home has for centuries been regarded as a "private" matter between the abuser, the victim and the immediate family. Women's organizations have been demanding for decades that domestic violence be treated as a crime and a violation of women's human rights.

All over the world, in every class, race and caste, in every religion and region, there are men who subject their intimate partners to physical or psychological violence, or both. Most violence against women is committed by the men they live with. The World Health Organization (WHO) says: "one of the most important risk factors for women – in terms of their vulnerability to sexual assault – is being married or cohabiting with a partner".[10] According to the WHO, refusing sex is one of the reasons women cite most often as a trigger for violence.[11]

For centuries, women have been told that men have the right to use violence against them, and many still believe it. Women in Hawaii describe such violence as "local love... more tough and a little more physical".[12] A 1999 study in South Africa discovered that more than a third of women believe that if a wife does something wrong her husband has a right to punish her.[13] And a husband's right to punish his wife is still enshrined in the Penal Code of Zamfara State, Northern Nigeria, in a section entitled "Correction of child, pupil, servant or wife".[14]

Murder in the family

Family killings are the only category of homicides where women outnumber men as victims. When a woman is killed in the home, it is her partner or male relative who is most likely to be the murderer. In 2001 the French Ministry of Health reported that on average six women a month die at the hands of their current or former partners.[16] In South Africa, the Medical Research Council calculates that on average a woman is killed by a current or former partner every six hours.[17] In El Salvador between September 2000 and December 2001, 134 women were murdered; an estimated 98 per cent were killed by their husbands or partners.[18]

The home is traditionally considered to be a safe haven. Yet this space where women in many societies spend a great deal of their time, and where they frequently object to the presence of weapons, exposes them to a particularly high risk of death when a gun is present. Most of the research available on what increases the risk of a woman being killed in the home has been conducted in countries of the North. Two recent studies from the USA show that:

▶ several factors affect a woman's chances of being killed by her husband or boyfriend, but *access to a gun* increases the risk five-fold;[19]

▶ *having a gun in the home* increased the overall risk of someone in the household being murdered by 41 per cent; but for women in particular the risk was nearly tripled (an increase of 272 per cent).[20]

The proportion of domestic homicides involving guns varies across the world. In South Africa and France, one in three women killed by their husbands is shot; in the USA this rises to two in three.[21]

Another study compared female homicide rates with gun ownership levels in 25 high-income countries, and found that where firearms are more available, more women are killed. In the USA, where there are high levels of gun ownership, women

A French investigating magistrate questions a man suspected of violence in the home. Women's activists around the world have established that violence against women is not a private issue but a human rights abuse. Governments, communities and individuals need to respond to violence in the home.

were at greater risk of homicide. The USA accounted for 32 per cent of the female population in these 25 countries, but for 70 per cent of all female homicides and 84 per cent of all women killed with firearms.[23]

Researchers for the South African Medical Research Council stated that in 1998 the rate of firearms episodes across three South African provinces was 10 times higher than in the USA, and that 150 in every 100,000 women aged between 18 and 49 in these provinces had been the victim of a firearms-related incident.

Thus the data show that the involvement of guns makes it far more likely that an attack will prove lethal. Why are guns so deadly in domestic assaults? One reason is the severity of the wounds caused by gunshot which is highly destructive of human tissue.[24] Another reason is that the presence of a firearm, with its threat of lethality, reduces a woman's capacity for resistance. The trauma of being threatened by a husband or partner is all the greater when he brandishes a gun and there is a very real danger of being killed. The wife of a US soldier told researchers: "He would say, 'You will do this, or...', and he would go to the gun cabinet".[25]

Guns also reduce the chances of victims escaping or of outsiders intervening to assist them. This was dramatically demonstrated on 7 August 2004, when 45-year old Marc Cécillon, five times French rugby captain, returned to a party held in his honour in his home town of Bourgoin-Jallieu near Lyon. Shortly before midnight, the hosts' teenage son reportedly saw Marc Cécillon coming up the driveway, tucking a pistol into the waistband of his shorts. The hosts' son ran to warn the guests, but he was too late. In the presence of 60 party-goers, Marc Cécillon approached the table where his wife Chantal was talking to friends and shot her four times with a .359 magnum, killing her instantly.[26]

Chantal Cécillon was killed in public, but the typical domestic killing occurs at the victim's home. Elizabeth Mhlongo of South Africa was shot dead in her bedroom in 1999, along with her five-year-old daughter Tlaleng. Her husband Solomon, a legal gun owner, emptied a magazine of bullets into the two victims, stopped to reload and then continued firing until the gun jammed. Elizabeth was left sprawled at the side of the bed, her chest, head, thigh and hand peppered with bullets, while Tlaleng lay slumped sideways in a blood-spattered chair.[27]

Preventing gun violence in the home

The small arms policies most likely to reduce the risk to women in their everyday lives are those that focus on how private individuals acquire guns and how they store them.

"Our research strongly supports the need for effective firearm control in South Africa as firearms are a very important weapon used to intimidate and injure women and facilitate rape."
South African Medical Research Council[29]

A superintendent of the Child Protection Unit in Johannesburg, South Africa, supports a 15-year-old rape survivor.

Several countries that have reformed their domestic gun laws over the past decade have begun to see the benefits, especially for women. Between 1995, when Canada tightened its gun laws, and 2003, the overall gun murder rate dropped by 15 per cent, while the gun homicide rate for women dropped by 40 per cent.[30] Likewise, for the five years after the gun laws in Australia were overhauled in 1996, the average gun murder rate was 45 per cent lower than it had been before the reforms. Again, the effect was more pronounced for female victims, with a drop of 57 per cent.[31]

Background checks to control the acquisition of weapons

US research shows that prior domestic violence in the household makes a woman far more likely to be a victim of family homicide.[32]

In most countries the law bans people with *serious criminal convictions* from buying or carrying guns. This usually means that when a person applies for a gun licence or tries to buy a gun, their criminal record is checked. However, such checks on their own are inadequate to stop abusive partners from acquiring guns because domestic violence so rarely results in convictions for a serious criminal offence. A vital part of overcoming the poor conviction rates is the existence of a criminal justice system that encourages women to report violence in the home, provides support for them when they do, and treats domestic violence as a serious offence. The reality is that in many countries women do not report violence in the home. Some are too fearful of their abusers to report them, others lack access to the police or justice system while others feel there is little point in reporting crimes which will not be taken seriously. A successful programme to stop gun violence in the home needs to address these wider issues of discrimination and violence against women.

Increasingly, countries are introducing restrictions to prevent gun licences being given to people who have had a *domestic violence protection order* issued against them. For example, the new Firearms Control Act in South Africa, which came into force in July 2004, specifies that a gun licence will be refused to anyone with a record of violence, including domestic violence.

Similarly, US federal law makes gun possession illegal for abusive husbands or partners who are subject to a restraining order or who have been convicted of a domestic violence misdemeanour.[33] Although this is an important measure to protect women, its effectiveness is undermined because criminal records are the responsibility of state governments and many states do not enter details of convictions for violence in the home into the federal database.[34] A further loophole that allows convicted criminals to acquire guns is that the federal law does not require any background checks to be made if the purchase is being made from an individual rather than from a federally licensed dealer. While some states have enacted complementary legislation imposing mandatory background checks for any arms sale, others have not, thus leaving a loophole for abusers wishing to buy guns. Individual sales account for around 40 per cent of all gun sales in the USA.[35]

Another way that the law can protect women from gun-related family violence is to allow the authorities to draw on a wide range of relevant information when deciding whether a gun licence should be granted. For example, Canadian gun law

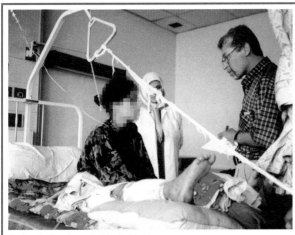

"He was very angry and he took his Kalashnikov... The neighbours said: 'Leave her alone'... But then he didn't stop; he shot my legs, I could not feel them, they were numb. The sun was setting, I was looking at the sky, I said to the men: 'I don't want to die.' They took me to the hospital."

Fatima in her hospital bed. © AI

Nineteen-year-old Fatima (not her real name) was shot in the legs by her husband in front of his family and their neighbours in Iraq on 21 May 2003. Married at the age of 12, she was treated as a servant and regularly beaten in her husband's family home. She tried to run away to her own family, but her husband came and said she should go back. When she refused he became very angry and took a piece of wood to beat her. It broke, so he grew even angrier and took out his gun and shot her.

Despite the number of eyewitnesses and the seriousness of the crime, neither the family nor the hospital reported the case to the police and her husband was not arrested. The family said it was a matter to be solved within the tribe. Fatima returned to her father's house after she left hospital. Her husband expressed regret and offered her compensation, seeking reconciliation with her through the mediation of elders of her tribe. However, she refused to return to him.[36]

requires the applicant's current or former spouse or partner to be notified before a licence is granted or renewed. The applicant also needs a reference, usually from their spouse or partner. The New Zealand police also have the power to seek the opinion of an applicant's current or past spouse. In Australia the opinion of the family doctor can be sought. While in Turkey applicants are required to provide a medical certificate attesting to their mental stability.

The need to disarm abusive partners

In Australia and in some US states it is compulsory for police to seize guns when a domestic violence protection order is issued – although sometimes the guns are returned shortly afterwards.

In South Africa, the Domestic Violence Act which came into force in 1999 gives police the power to remove weapons from an alleged abuser at the victim's request. In research undertaken in the Cape Town area, the authors of a 2001 report noted that "very few weapons are ordered to be removed when compared with the number of times weapons are mentioned in the applicants' affidavits". The authors suggested that the form used is complicated and unclear, but that also most police officers are not motivated to try and do not take violence against women as seriously as they should. As one police officer interviewed said: "You do have to confiscate weapons, but not that often. Yes there are complaints that the husband has threatened to shoot her, but he never does. It's never serious."[37]

Provisions for disarming abusive husbands or partners depend on the existence of a robust firearm registration system. Registration is especially important for protecting victims of violence in the home. This was demonstrated in New South Wales, Australia, in 1992 when Kerry Anne Gannan took out a restraining order against her former partner, Malcolm Baker, for domestic violence. The law required police to cancel Malcolm Baker's gun licence and remove his guns; but in the absence of a registration system they had no way of knowing how many guns he had. The police searched his house and found five guns, which they assumed to be the extent of his arsenal. However, Malcolm Baker had another gun which the police did not find. He used it to kill six people including Kerry Anne Gannan and her sister, who was eight months pregnant. This was not a case where the claim of domestic violence had been treated lightly, but the efforts of the police were undermined by the lack of registration.[38]

Storing weapons safely

The availability of guns in the home can also be affected by the storage conditions prescribed in gun laws. Countries such as Australia, Canada, Japan and the UK require gun owners to store the gun securely and to keep the ammunition in a separate place. In Belarus guns must be kept in locked boxes, disassembled and unloaded, with the ammunition stored separately.[39] Another measure that has been proposed by women's groups is a ban on keeping guns in private homes, at least in urban or suburban areas. The idea is that guns would be stored in secure storage facilities that comply with certain gun safety standards – for example at an authorized gun club or police station – from where their owners could retrieve them for hunting or sport.

Australia tackles use of guns in family violence

One of the primary aims of the Australian firearms law reforms in the 1990s was to stop guns being used in violence in the home.[40] The following were among the specific measures introduced to tackle the use of guns in domestic violence.

▶ Gun ownership requires a licence, obtained by meeting a series of criteria including a minimum age of 18, a clean criminal record, being a "fit and proper person", undergoing safety training and proving "genuine reason".

▶ When deciding whether to grant or renew a licence, police can take into account all relevant circumstances.

▶ People convicted of assault are banned from having a gun licence for at least five years.

▶ People subject to domestic violence restraining orders are banned from having a gun licence for five years.

▶ People with domestic violence restraining orders against them are subject to compulsory seizure of all their guns.

▶ All guns must be registered at time of sale and when the licence is renewed.

▶ There is a 28-day waiting period to buy a gun.

▶ "Genuine reason" must be proved separately for each gun, effectively imposing a limit on the number of guns that any one person can own.

▶ Guns cannot be bought and sold privately, but only through licensed dealers or the police.

▶ There are strict requirements on how guns must be stored.

An evaluation of the Australian reforms published in October 2004 found that the laws had produced dramatic reductions in firearm-related deaths.[41]

Women taking action – campaigning for gun control

Million Mom March

In August 1999 a gunman randomly shot a group of children in Granada Hill, California, USA. In the wake of the shootings Donna Dees-Thomases launched an appeal for women to gather outside the White House in Washington on Mother's Day 2000 to demand that Congress pass gun control legislation. She and other organizers expected 100,000 people to turn up. Over 750,000 demonstrators gathered in Washington, while simultaneously a further 60 marches took place across the country.

The Million Mom March has joined with the Brady Campaign to Prevent Gun Violence, set up after Jim Brady, then press secretary to President Ronald Reagan, was shot and seriously wounded during an assassination attempt on the President in 1981.

Mothers Against Guns

"School shootings, workplace shootings, church shootings, drive-by shootings – when does it stop? Who enforces the law when a police officer shoots an unarmed person? Is justice blind in our society?... Cowards are committing these crimes, and we are cowards for allowing them to do it".

Liz Bishop-Goldsmith, founder of Mothers Against Guns USA[42]

Mothers Against Guns USA was established in New York in 1994 by Liz Bishop-Goldsmith after she lost two young members of her family to gun violence. It campaigns actively with local councils for firearms and ammunition controls.

Gun Free South Africa

"We felt the biggest threat to our new democracy was the surplus weapons of war that had saturated our country".

Adele Kirsten, a peace and anti-militarization campaigner and one of the founders of Gun Free South Africa

Gun Free South Africa (GFSA) was established in 1994, the same year as South Africa's first democratic elections. GFSA was one of the civil society organizations that lobbied successfully for tough gun controls. The reaction from some gun owners to GFSA's support for the Firearms Control Act has been vitriolic. Adele Kirsten says: "it is the women in particular in GFSA who bear the brunt of what appears to be white male rage. We are targeted with the abusive phone calls, the name-calling whether it be on public radio or in the press, often with an implicit violence – all this because we are seen as taking away their guns. It is not pleasant but what it tells us is that we are challenging deep issues here of sexual and gender identity, the core of colonial white male identity."[43]

What needs to be done?

a State authorities, armed groups, and political, community and religious leaders should publicly denounce violence against women whenever and wherever it occurs. They should make it clear that such violence is a violation of women's human rights and will not be tolerated.

b States should ensure that violence against women is prohibited in national law as a criminal offence with effective penalties for perpetrators and remedies for survivors, and that these laws are fully implemented.

c States should halt gun proliferation by making it compulsory for anyone who wants to own a gun to get a licence. In line with the best practice worldwide, licences should only be issued by government authorities in accordance with strict criteria that exclude the granting of licences to those with a history of violence in the home or community, and which take into account the declared reasons for requesting a licence, the context in which the application is made and the likelihood of misuse.

d States should treat family violence as a serious crime on a par with assaults in other contexts, and in a way that protects and supports women who report it.

Chapter 3
Law enforcers, guns and violence against women

Young women in the Solomon Islands holding up placards with the slogan 'the time for guns is finished now', 2003.

3: Law enforcers, guns and violence against women

Law enforcement officials – police, immigration, customs and other security officials, border guards and sometimes paramilitary and military personnel – are given special powers to use force and firearms where necessary. The circumstances in which law enforcement officials may use force and the level of force they may use are set out in international human rights standards (see Chapter 7).[44] Unfortunately, many states have not incorporated these into their national law, let alone implemented them in practice.

Law enforcement officials often wield powers and use guns in violation of international standards, including by committing violence against women. Such human rights violations are more likely to occur:

▸ if those responsible for gun misuse are not brought to justice;

▸ if law enforcement officials receive poor training and inappropriate equipment; and

▸ if there is a widespread lack of respect for the human rights of women.

In combination these factors can increase the risk that law enforcement officials will ignore gun crime against women and use guns to abuse women.

Most police and other law enforcers who are armed or who have easy access to firearms and other weapons are men. Police and other law enforcers have a legal monopoly on the use of violence in non-war situations. This gives them great responsibility and power as well as the potential for serious abuses.

"I was 14 years old then. One of the policemen came one night around 10pm, pointed a gun at me and ordered me to follow him to see the other men... The Commander... pointed his gun at me and raped me. I suffered pain and bleeding."

A woman from the Solomon Islands[45]

Misusing guns against women

Law enforcement officers who use their position to carry out armed violence against women represent a fundamental betrayal of the obligations states have to protect women within their jurisdiction.[46]

Law enforcement officers who are authorized to take their weapons home pose a particular risk to women. If there are no rigorous procedures in place to store law enforcers' weapons securely at their place of work, there is a risk that the officers may misuse their guns while off duty.

When police officers and other law enforcers use their firearms to commit sexual violence against women, many women fear that any resistance could cost them their lives. A group of schoolgirls who had attended the annual agricultural show in Nairobi, Kenya, missed the school bus home. According to reports, they took a taxi into the centre of town; it was nearly 8.30pm, and they agreed they would ask help from the first police officer they met. "Soon they spotted a group of police officers and rushed to them and narrated their story. The officers seemed willing to help and told the girls to follow them to a nearby church where they would request accommodation for them. But the church grounds [turned out to be] a recreation garden. The kind officers' mood changed, and at gunpoint they raped the three girls in turn."[47]

Regular police and paramilitary officers also commit armed violence against women in situations of civil disturbance that evolve into and out of armed conflict. In the Solomon Islands during the five-year armed conflict (1998-2003), ethnic militias, regular police and special constables raped and otherwise tortured many women and girls. Some women were forced into sexual slavery. In 2003, an Australian-led Pacific police force, backed by soldiers, began an operation aimed at restoring law and order in the Solomon Islands. Some 3,500 people were arrested as part of the operation. However, many women who had suffered sexual violence did not pursue their cases through the courts, often because they feared that their abuser would seek revenge or that their male relatives would object. In 2004, AI delegates interviewed 55 women and girls living in Weathercoast on Guadalcanal Island. Nineteen said that they had been raped by armed forces occupying or raiding their village; most were teenagers and the youngest was 11 years old.[48]

Soldiers performing policing duties are often not professionally trained to act as law enforcement officials and lack accountability. In such situations there is a heightened risk of armed violence against women. In some cases armed sexual violence against women may be used as a tool to repress popular resistance. For example, women living in the Niger Delta, an area at the centre of Nigeria's profitable oil industry, have campaigned for better environmental protection and greater access to the wealth generated. Since 1994, when the military government set up a military task force to deal with protests in the Delta, women have faced violence, including shootings and rape by army personnel.[49]

Taking violence against women seriously

The criminal justice system is the key institution that should reflect a state's recognition of the seriousness of violence against women, and its determination to protect women under its jurisdiction. But too often women subjected to armed violence at home do not receive the help they need from the police. A culture that tolerates men using violence against women and the fact that most police officers are men, make it difficult for women to approach the police for help.

"You call the police... And they tell him, 'Oh come on, you know. Women get cranky.'... blah blah blah. And to me, they were saying, 'Why don't you stop upsetting him? Make him a nice dinner and get off his back'... And so they'd leave you with a wild man."
A woman in Hawaii[50]

In Afghanistan, women told AI that any woman experiencing violence at home who sought outside help would run the very real risk of being murdered if she were found out. A woman in Nangarhar Province said, "a woman would be killed [if she sought help] because it is the Pashtun Wali [customary law] tradition and because it is a big shame if a woman brings her problems outside the home."

Women's and human rights organizations are campaigning for governments to treat violence in the family as a serious crime and enable police forces to take action against suspected abusers. These campaigns have achieved some successes. For example, in the USA, with support from women's rights campaigners, federal legislators re-authorized the Violence Against Women Act in 2000, thus providing continued funding for a wide array of activities to prevent violence against women, including training for law enforcement officers.

But in countries around the world some police officers continue to ignore the gravity of the crimes committed against women, and deal with the perpetrators "man to man". Researchers from the Cape Town Consortium on Violence Against Women in South Africa found in the police and justice sector "an alarming number of interviewees who identified more closely with the circumstances of the respondent than with those of the complainant." The report continued: "This may be attributable to the fact that most criminal justice personnel are male."[52]

A counsellor at the Saartjie Baartman shelter for battered women in Cape Town, South Africa, told researchers there had been cases where women in the shelter had applied to have a firearm removed from their partner, but "then the abuser tells the police that he needs the gun for work and he gets it back".[53]

The UN has highlighted the importance of ensuring that law enforcement agencies are representative and responsive to the community as a whole (see Chapter 7). However, it appears that most police selection, recruitment and career structures do not meet this standard with regard to women (or to other parts of the community, such as ethnic minorities). Moreover, in some countries, rather than fully integrating female officers into all parts of the police service, there is a tendency to deploy them to clerical roles or units which specialize in domestic violence and child abuse, regardless of their skills or suitability for such work.

Women taking action – changing attitudes

There are, however, some examples of progress being made. In Bosnia-Herzegovina, Medica Infoteka, which was established by women during the war, provides integrated support services to women in Bosnia-Herzegovina. It is working to change the entire country's attitudes towards domestic violence, starting with the police and judges. Director Duska Andric-Ruzicic described the work of the group: "We didn't go in there telling them how to do their job; just told them we're trying to show them a new point of view – that of the victim". Now in at least one municipality, only certain designated police officers deal with abused women. "This is revolutionary", she says. "Women no longer have to tell their often difficult stories to an assembly line of untrained officers. The police have said they're proud to be part of this effort. Other municipalities are asking for training too."[54]

What needs to be done?

a Governments should issue clear instructions to all law enforcement personnel that all forms of violence against women are prohibited and a violation of human rights.

b States should promote and publicize UN human rights standards for law enforcers, including those on the use of force. And they should incorporate these standards into law and practice.

c Governments should overhaul recruitment and training policies in law enforcement agencies so that they become organizations that are representative of, responsive to and accountable to the community as a whole.

d Law enforcement authorities should suspend any official suspected of involvement in violence against women while the allegations against them are investigated, and bring to justice law enforcement personnel responsible for violence against women in procedures which meet international standards of fairness.

Chapter 4
Gangs, guns and gender

Young boys with guns in Rio de Janeiro, Brazil, 2002.

4: Gangs, guns and gender

Armed gang violence is mostly a male phenomenon. The main perpetrators and victims are young men. But women are also affected when public space, whether it be urban streets or rural fields, becomes a dangerous place because of the activities of armed gangs.

Armed gang violence exposes everyone in the community, irrespective of gender, to the risk of being injured or killed in the crossfire. But when a culture of armed gang violence takes root in a society that fails to respect women's rights, the result is a higher level of gender-based violence against women. In this situation, the proliferation of guns increases the risks that girls and women will be the targets of violent attacks, especially sexual assault.

The actions of armed gangs can also shape public spaces for women. If armed gangs are on the street and they are known to attack and rape women, then getting to work, and going about their daily lives become dangerous for women. The restrictions, fear and danger that women and girls experience in such situations are intensified by the uncontrolled proliferation of firearms. This danger is clearly increased when gangs are wielding automatic and semi-automatic military specification firearms which can fire many rounds in rapid succession. Moreover, the bullets fired from many types of assault weapons are designed to pass through humans and also through structures, and therefore pose a heightened risk of hitting passers-by.

"My job is crime... I have bought my house from the money I made from robberies. I respect crime. It looks after me."

Gang member in Papua New Guinea[55]

Guns ratchet up the level of violence against women

In South Africa, where the phenomenon of armed gangs is well established, 14 per cent of sexual assaults are reported to be committed with firearms – far higher than for neighbouring countries.[56]

Gang membership has knock-on effects for women in violent relationships. Counsellors say a woman will hesitate to apply for a firearm to be taken away from her partner if he is a member of a gang: "If the police take the abuser's gun, then the abuser's friends will come after her. Because of this fear of retribution within the gang, women often do not file for gun removals from gang members".[57]

"The pervasiveness of gang rape as a form of criminal activity had become a major threat to the security of women throughout Papua New Guinea."

A 1998 study by UNICEF

Women in Papua New Guinea are frequently victims of armed crime, including sexual assault, perpetrated by members of armed gangs. With urban unemployment rates estimated to range from 60 to 90 per cent, armed gangs provide employment for growing numbers of unemployed youths and men.[58]

In Malawi between 1997 and 1999, the number of armed robberies of urban and rural homes and businesses reported to the police rose by nearly 40 per cent.[59] Armed gangs obtained AK47 semi-automatic rifles from stocks left over from the war in Mozambique and from imports via Zambia and Tanzania. They also obtained government-issue firearms from the Malawi police and army.[60] A culture of weaponry became attractive to young men and boys and some formed vigilante groups.[61] In the worst affected areas, girls and women were sometimes sexually attacked or robbed, and had to be escorted to schools, places of work, shops and wells.[62]

In Iraq, the US-led invasion and occupation have given rise to high levels of violence and human rights abuses. The general lawlessness which engulfed large parts of the country following the invasion put women and girls at increased risk of violence. Reports suggest that as a result of the increase in the number of sexual

"They were armed, they put guns to my head and said 'come with us'. I screamed and said take the pistol away. My daughter started to scream. They pulled my hair and pushed me in the car and started shooting at the house."

Salma, aged 49, from Iraq. She managed to get away the next day, but only after she had been brutally raped and tortured by 10 men.[63]

Women taking action – from survivors to advocates

"From one day to the next, my dreams were shattered – all because of the irresponsibility of supposedly civilized men who only feel brave with a gun in their hands".

Camila Magalhães Lima, Brazil[64]

© Viva Rio

Camila Magalhães Lima was walking home from school when she was hit by a bullet fired during a shoot-out between a gang of armed robbers and a private security firm. She lost the use of her legs. She now campaigns against gun violence in Brazil.

At the end of 2002, 18-year-old Charlene Ellis and 17-year-old Letisha Shakespeare had stepped out of a New Year's Eve party in Aston, UK, for some fresh air when they were caught in a hail of bullets and killed. Charlene's twin sister Sophie was injured. The women in their families were moved to begin campaigning against the lethal consequences of gun and gang culture in their community, setting up Safer Lives Safer Communities, which works with The Disarm Trust, a national organization. Sandra Shakespeare, Letisha's aunt, says one of the biggest changes is going to take time – and that involves men themselves and how they bring up children. "Men should stand up and take responsibility… Learn how to walk and hold your head up high and say this is the true way to be a man."[65]

assaults and rapes in Baghdad, many women are now afraid to leave their homes. The ready availability of guns has facilitated a rise in violent attacks, and in particular abductions, by criminal gangs. Following the fall of the government of Saddam Hussein in April 2003, an estimated seven to eight million firearms were looted from military and police premises, many of them automatic and semi-automatic assault weapons.[66]

Changing attitudes

"The women do not fire AK-47 rifles. However they have an important cultural role in cattle rustling. The weapon they have is their tongue."

A female commentator on the role of women in encouraging armed violence in pastoral regions of Uganda[68]

There are many reasons why men carry guns in public. But one of them, as UK Home Office Minister Carolyn Flint pointed out in July 2003, is that: "Young people, almost always men and often linked to gangs, petty crime and illegal drugs, increasingly carry guns as a means of gaining respect."[67]

Girls' and young women's attitudes can encourage this aspect of gun-holding, by continuing to see men as having greater status if they carry guns. Interviews with girls and young women in *favelas* (shanty towns) in Rio de Janeiro, Brazil, show how young men who carry guns to participate in the drug trade represent status, money and power: "Girls go out with guys who use guns because they want a good life, easy money, brand-name clothes, feel superior to others... have power over others... If she goes out with a regular working guy her life won't be like that. She likes going out with traffickers for that reason."[69]

The ambiguous role played by women in the Karamoja pastoralist region of north-eastern Uganda means that they can be advocates for peace in their communities while at the same time encouraging men to go out on the armed cattle-rustling raids which have brought such insecurity to communities in the region.

"You could do prevention strategies, intervention strategies, you could lock up the two main gangs and every other gang member what you have on the database and it is still going to be here, because it is a culture. You can't arrest a culture, you can't lock up a mindset. You need to get rid of that mindset from society."

Mark Edwards, a community activist who spent several years working with gang members in the UK, 2004[70]

The importance of women's and girls' roles in influencing male gun ownership and use has been recognized by the Brazilian non-governmental organization Viva Rio. In 2001 the Rio de Janeiro-based organization decided to involve "mothers, sisters, girlfriends, wives and cousins" in a campaign to force young men to give up their guns. The campaign uses women's activism to spread the message that, contrary to cultural and media messages, guns do not make a man more manly or attractive. The idea is to "de-masculinize" the gun, using puns suggesting that a man's potency is reduced if he carries a gun.

The factors fuelling organized violence in the community are varied and complex and can be related to economic inequality, social injustice, the growth of organized

crime, and the power of the globalized market-place. Such factors need to be addressed if gang violence is to be eradicated, but they lie beyond the scope of this report. One of the most important tasks, however, is to convince young men that they do not need to have a gun in order to gain respect.

Civil society has an important role to play in changing attitudes towards guns and ensuring that governments do not perpetrate human rights violations while working to eradicate crime. Guiding principles for work at the community level to reduce gun violence are set out in Appendix 2. Young people need to be offered alternative ways to make a living and to spend their leisure time. They need to have access to alternative role models that are not based on equating masculinity with armed violence and associating femininity with passivity and objectification.[71]

Basra, southern Iraq, April 2003. With increased numbers of arms in circulation in Iraq since the US-led invasion in 2003, issues of protection for women have become paramount.

Colombian soldiers keep a close eye on a human rights demonstration organized by the Popular Women's Organization, 1998.

The **We Can** campaign, the South Asia regional campaign to end violence against women, was launched in September 2004. It seeks to achieve a fundamental shift in social attitudes and beliefs that support violence against women. It is based on the belief that women and girls have a right to a life free from violence and that, if all sections of society accept responsibility and act, together we can end all violence against women.

The **We Can** campaign aims to reach and influence 50 million ordinary men and women across six countries of South Asia to oppose violence against women and adopt more gender equal practices in their own lives. To achieve this aim, over five million "change makers" – people who will work to influence men and women – will be mobilized through a series of highly visible and coordinated mobilization programmes at a local, national and regional level.

Equal relationships are violence free. Together, we can end all violence against women.

Find out more at http://www.wecanendvaw.org

What needs to be done?

a Governments, local authorities and civil society organizations should mobilize official resources and community structures to help develop sustainable livelihoods in order to address the social and economic roots of armed gang violence and provide alternative role models of masculinity and femininity.

b Governments and local authorities, in partnership with civil society and police, should develop participatory community safety programmes that promote practical ways of halting the violence arising from the proliferation and misuse of guns and address its specific impact on women and girls.

c States should ban private individuals from owning military specification assault weapons, other than in the most exceptional circumstances consistent with respect for human rights.

d States should act with due diligence to prevent and investigate violent criminal acts which infringe women's right to life, liberty, dignity and security of the person; bring to justice those responsible for such crimes; ensure reparation for survivors; and take steps to curb proliferation of small arms in the community.

Chapter 5
Crimes against women in armed conflict

Kula, aged 47, was gang-raped by members of an armed opposition group. She was photographed at a camp for internally displaced people in Monrovia, Liberia, in August 2003.

5: Crimes against women in armed conflict

"Civilians, particularly women and children, account for the vast majority of those adversely affected by armed conflict, including as refugees and internally displaced persons, and increasingly are targeted by combatants and armed elements."

UN Security Council[72]

In recent years armed groups have committed war crimes and crimes against humanity, including mass rape, against women in all regions of the world. Between March 1999 and February 2000, the Sierra Leone Chapter of the Forum for African Women Educationalists (FAWE) helped and supported more than 2,000 women and girls who had been abducted by armed combatants. These were mostly women and girls from Freetown and the Western Area. More than 1,900 of them had been raped. Most had sexually transmitted diseases, and many were pregnant; 80 per cent of those who were pregnant were between 14 and 18 years old.[73]

International law prohibits governments and armed groups from targeting civilians. International instruments also set out the steps governments should take to protect women from gender-based violence in times of conflict (see Chapter 7). But the reality for women and girls is that war comes to their homes, their businesses, their fields, the schools they teach or study in, the hospitals where they practise, and the clinics they go to for health care.

In many modern conflicts the vast majority of those subjected to violence are civilians; the majority of civilians are women and children. For example, in September and October 2004, four Palestinian schoolgirls were shot dead by the Israeli army in their classrooms or walking to school in the Gaza Strip. Among them was Iman al-Hams who was shot dead by Israeli soldiers near her school in Rafah on 5 October. Exceptionally, this case received considerable attention after soldiers testified to the media that their company commander repeatedly shot Iman al-Hams from close range when she was already lying on the ground. Charges brought against the commander included illegal use of his weapon, but not murder or manslaughter.[74] In another incident on 2 May 2004, Tali Hatuel, a 34-year-old Israeli woman in her eighth month of pregnancy, and her four young daughters were killed by Palestinian gunmen as they were travelling by car in the Gaza Strip. They were shot dead at close range and rescue workers said the children had bullet wounds to the head.[75]

Women are also targeted as peace activists, as mediators and negotiators in conflict, and as human rights defenders and humanitarian aid workers. And while the increasing international focus on sexual violence committed in the context of conflict is a necessary and important development, it is also important to remember the many other aspects of women's experience of arms and conflict.

The social and economic impact of armed conflict on women

Conflict often results in mass movements of the civilian populations as people are forced to flee their homes. This has a disproportionate impact on women since most of

the world's displaced people are women and children. At the same time other factors – such as their care responsibilities and social restrictions on their mobility – mean that women are less able to flee when the civilian population comes under attack and so are at greater risk of abuse by combatants. Armed groups and governments put limits on people's movement – setting up armed checkpoints and closing borders – creating situations where women are at particular risk of sexual violence.

When armed groups and soldiers raid communities for food and supplies, destroy or poison their foodstocks or water, or prevent people moving around freely, or making a living, this also has a disproportionate impact on women. This is in large part because the burden of managing and providing for the household, caring for the

Women protesters in Liberia's capital, Monrovia, in 2003 calling for peace and for help from the UN to end killings and rape.

elderly, for children and for people with disabilities frequently falls on women during conflict, especially when male relatives are more directly involved in fighting or are detained, injured or killed.[76]

Sexual crimes against women during conflict

"At night the other soldiers raped me. They came almost every night. They said that the more they raped me, the more they would be men, and the higher up the ranks they would rise".

Sange, who enlisted as a child soldier in the DRC with one armed group when she was 10, and was then abducted by another group[77]

Small arms and light weapons are often used by combatants to wreak havoc in the lives of women. They facilitate sexual violence against women and girls. Sometimes the sexual violence is opportunistic; sometimes it is used as a deliberate military and political tactic.

In the course of the armed conflict in eastern Democratic Republic of Congo (DRC), tens of thousands of women and girls have been raped and sexually assaulted by combatant forces. Women and girls have been attacked in their homes, in the fields, or as they go about their other daily activities. Many have been raped more than once or have survived gang rapes. Girl child soldiers have also been the victims of rape and sexual violence.

Rape has often been accompanied by other forms of torture. Caroline, who is 15 years old, and her mother were abducted on the way to their fields and held captive for two months in 2003. "Each morning, noon and evening, [the soldiers] would put us in the same house, force us to lie on the ground and then they would rape us, all in the same room. While they were doing this, they were hitting and kicking us in the stomach, back and face. My mother's hand was broken; it is still swollen and she can't use it. My buttocks are still painful and I can't use my arm any more. There were twelve soldiers."[78]

Women and girl combatants

The prevalence of small arms that are affordable and easy to carry and use has changed the landscape of warfare, allowing women and children to be recruited as combatants. Women are now recruited as a matter of course by the armed forces of many countries. Women and girls are also abducted into armed groups, or choose to join them, sometimes as a reaction to abuses they have suffered at the hands of state forces. These developments have drawn women and girls ever closer into the violence of conflict, sometimes placing them in the ambiguous position of being simultaneously the perpetrators and victims of violence.[79]

In Nepal, where government forces and the Communist Party of Nepal-Maoist (CPN-Maoist) have been locked in conflict since 1996, around a third of

CPN-Maoist combatants in Rukum District, Nepal, April 2004. It is estimated that a third of the armed group's combatants are women.

CPN-Maoist combatants are believed to be women. Both state forces and the CPN-Maoists have committed human rights abuses, including torture and killings of civilians.

The majority of women in Nepal have traditionally participated in the public sphere only through their fathers and husbands, and have suffered social, legal and cultural discrimination. The CPN-Maoist has capitalized on this, and attracted women into their armed forces by promising greater gender equality. Kamala Roka, District President of the Maoist Women's Wing, told the *Nepali Times*: "The People's War has emboldened us women, it has given us confidence, and we are treated equally. However, once in a while you do see male dominance in our movement."[80]

It is not only women who can end up in fighting forces, but girls too. According to the Coalition to Stop the Use of Child Soldiers, girls are involved in armed conflict in most regions of the world.[81] Hundreds of girls were among the thousands of children recruited as soldiers after conflict resumed in Liberia in 1999. All parties to the conflict – the former government, and the two armed opposition groups, Liberians United for Reconciliation and Democracy (LURD) and the Movement for Democracy in Liberia (MODEL) – abducted children, both girls and boys, and forced them to fight, carry ammunition, prepare food or do other tasks. Girls were raped and forced to provide sexual services, and girls and women were actively engaged in fighting.

Women can also support human rights abuses by men. For example, in Bosnia-Herzegovina, women have been as susceptible as men to racist or xenophobic ideologies. Bosnian women taken from their homes in Foča in 1992 reported that amongst the well-armed Bosnian-Serb forces who took them to the Partizan Sports Hall were women soldiers. The Sports Hall was one of the primary locations used by Serb forces in Foča to carry out systematic rapes of hundreds of Bosnian women. Women held there were raped dozens, if not hundreds, of times.[83] In Miljevina, a village within the Foča municipality, certain local women allegedly organized the abduction of non-Serb women from their houses and their imprisonment in locations where they were raped repeatedly.[84]

Women taking action for peace

In conflicts around the world, women have organized themselves at the grassroots level to promote peace. Despite this, they are frequently excluded from formal peace negotiations and peacebuilding initiatives.

In the Solomon Islands, Women for Peace emerged in 2000 out of women's efforts to stop nearly five years of fighting between ethnic militias. In an environment where sexual violence against women was a very real danger, the group met and prayed together at the frontline and then headed out to the "bunkers" to ask the young men and boys to lay down their weapons. Some young men reportedly burst into tears when the women spoke to them, but others threatened them with violence. Despite a Women's Communique for Peace issued in May 2000, no women's groups were invited to participate in the negotiations that led to the Townsville Peace Agreement in October 2000. In December 2000, parliament passed a blanket amnesty for almost all crimes and atrocities committed during the conflict, including violence against women.[85]

What needs to be done?

a All parties to armed conflicts should publicly condemn violence against women and ensure that their forces abide by the laws of war. In particular, they should put in place safeguards and training to stop the sexual abuse of women and girls that has characterized so many conflicts.

b All parties to armed conflicts should make their combatants fully aware of their duty to refuse manifestly illegal orders, specifically orders to commit crimes of violence against women and other human rights abuses.

c Military authorities should suspend any armed forces members suspected of involvement in violence against women while the allegations against them are investigated, and bring to justice those responsible for violence against women, in proceedings which meet international standards of fair trial.

d States should cooperate in bringing those suspected of perpetrating violence against women to justice, whether through their own courts or through international tribunals and the International Criminal Court.

e States should respect and enforce arms embargoes to prevent the transfer of arms into conflict zones where they could contribute to violence against women and other human rights abuses.

"I saw young people being kidnapped. I saw women being raped and girls being raped. There was a feeling in me that I have to do something to restore peace, and it was up to us to do it. No one else was going to do it."

Martha Horiwapu, trauma and torture counsellor, Women for Peace, Solomon Islands[86]

An Acehnese woman walks past an Indonesian security forces checkpoint in north Nanggroe Aceh Darussalam, Indonesia, November 2002.

Chapter 6
The aftermath of war

6: The aftermath of war

Widespread, unregulated access to small arms and ammunition following ceasefire and peace agreements facilitates further armed violence against women. One of the most important tasks in the aftermath of conflict is disarming former combatants and reintegrating them into society. But disarmament, demobilization and reintegration programmes have often failed to cater for the needs of women and girls. This is especially true of women and girls who were used by fighting groups for sex and domestic tasks, but did not carry guns themselves and so have been excluded from such programmes as not "real combatants". This is another example of the effects of the under-representation of women in official peace-making, peacekeeping and peace-building initiatives, even when such initiatives are backed by the international community.

The brutalizing effects of war

The brutalizing effects of armed conflict do not disappear with the end of conflict. For returning combatants, both women and men, the transition from the violence of the frontline to home life can be extremely problematic. The return of male relatives, many traumatized and brutalized by the conflict, can bring violence directly into the home.

If men bring weapons home with them, the danger to women increases. A study in Northern Ireland showed that the increased availability of guns meant that more dangerous forms of violence were used against women in the home.[87] SOS-Belgrade reported that men came back from fighting traumatized, angry and violent, and used the weapons they brought with them to threaten or harm women.[88]

In vast areas of Afghanistan, where regional and local commanders and their armed groups still wield arbitrary and unchecked power, women and girls face a high risk of rape and sexual violence from the members of these armed factions and former combatants. Their attempts both to engage in political activity and to ensure the integration of women's rights in the process of reconstruction have been obstructed. Women in Mazar-e-Sharif and Jalalabad told AI representatives in April and May 2003 that the insecurity and fear of sexual violence made their lives worse than during the Taleban era. Women also said the general insecurity was being used by male family members to justify imposing further restrictions on their movements.[90] "If the situation gets worse, my father says we should not go to school", said a young woman in Kabul.[91]

Governments, leaders of armed opposition groups, and international bodies need to agree mechanisms to ensure the collection and destruction of surplus and illegal weapons in the context of peace agreements. To do this effectively women's and other civilian community organizations must be fully involved in the peace process and in monitoring disarmament programmes.

Demobilizing and reintegrating women and girls

Disarmament, demobilization and reintegration is the official process of collecting weapons from former combatants, taking combatants out of a military structure and helping them to move back into civilian life. Women and girl soldiers trying to reintegrate into society have particular needs. This may be because of social attitudes which, for example, result in the rejection of women who have been raped or sexually abused. Or it may be because of the abuses they have suffered. For example, women and girls who have been recruited as "wives" of combatants need to be given an alternative to accompanying their captors – the men who have raped and abused them – to cantonment sites to await demobilization.

Yet until very recently, as the UN Secretary-General has acknowledged, many programmes failed to take the needs of women and girl combatants into account.[93] Fighting forces are sometimes reluctant to admit the very existence of women combatants and in particular girl child soldiers. In addition, when access to disarmament, demobilization and reintegration programmes is dependent on handing in a gun, girl soldiers may be excluded because they were not given guns but instead forced to work as cooks and porters and to provide sex.

In Sierra Leone, approximately 30 per cent of the child soldiers in rebel forces were girls.[94] Yet between 1998 and 2002 only eight per cent of the 6,900 children who were formally demobilized in the country were girls.[95]

However, some progress has been made. In Liberia, the disarmament, demobilization and reintegration programme designed by UN agencies and others did in principle recognize the difficulties facing demobilized girls and women and made specific arrangements to address them. For example:

▶ it provided for separate demobilization camps, or separate areas within camps;

▶ it aimed to involve a network of women's organizations with expertise in counselling victims of sexual violence, in reproductive health and in psycho-social support;

▶ it specified that access to health care, basic education, skills training and personal development counselling must be provided for girl and women ex-combatants.

"Women are in a bad situation here... Mothers are afraid. They are worried about their daughters – that the armed men will do something to the girls."
A woman in Faizabad, Afghanistan[92]

"After more than 10 years of conflict, there are men and women, and unfortunately also children, who have known only violence... The real danger is, if they remain idle, they can regroup not only to destabilize Liberia but the whole of the sub-region."
Independent Expert on Liberia, Charlotte Abaka, appointed by the UN Commission on Human Rights, July 2004[96]

45

After an abortive start in December 2003, the programme resumed in mid-April 2004, eight months after the former government of Liberia, LURD and MODEL had signed a peace agreement.[97] By 31 October 2004, when the disarmament and demobilization programme was officially declared to be over, some 96,000 combatants had been disarmed – far more than the initial estimate of 53,000. They included more than 17,000 women and some 9,250 children, both girls and boys. A serious deficiency in the funds provided by the international community for rehabilitation and reintegration programmes jeopardized the prospects of effectively meeting the particular needs of women former combatants. In September 2004 the UN Secretary-General and the UN Security Council urgently called on the international community to contribute generously towards programmes for reintegration and rehabilitation.[98] Liberia's traumatized population is at risk of further violence if former combatants, including women and girls, are not given adequate assistance to resume civilian life and give up their guns.

Women and peace building

In 2000, following campaigning from the women's rights movement, the UN Security Council passed Resolution 1325. This **Resolution on Women, Peace and Security** is a historic step that acknowledges the essential role of women in peace building. It calls for the full inclusion of women in decision-making at all levels, in the prevention, management, and resolution of conflict, and in peace processes. It refers to women's involvement in UN field-based operations and especially among military observers, civilian police and human rights and humanitarian personnel. It calls for the particular needs of women and girls to be considered in the design of refugee camps, in repatriation and resettlement, in mine clearance, in post-conflict reconstruction and in disarmament, demobilization and reintegration programmes.

However, much needs to be done if the principles of Resolution 1325 are to become a reality. For example, UNIFEM, a UN agency, mandated to provide financial and technical assistance to promote women's human rights, political participation and economic security, remains the smallest UN fund. In the four years after the adoption of Resolution 1325, less than 20 per cent of UN Security Council resolutions included any reference to women or gender.[99] Following worldwide campaigning by women, peace and human rights groups, on 28 October 2004, the UN Security Council adopted a UN-wide action plan to implement Resolution 1325 and to fully integrate a gender perspective into conflict prevention and peacekeeping work.[100]

Women taking action – involvement in peace processes

From April 2003, women in Liberia began a Mass Action for Peace campaign, drawing in women from all faiths and levels of society. While the parties to the conflict were negotiating a peace agreement in Ghana from June 2003, the women took the Mass Action to Accra, bodily confining the delegates in the hall and blocking the entrance when leaders of one of the armed opposition groups threatened to walk out. As a result of their campaign, women gained entry to key meetings. A delegation of Liberian women from the Mano River Women Peace Network (MARWOPNET) took part in the talks, and was one of the groups representing civil society that signed the peace agreement in August 2003 as witnesses.[101]

What needs to be done?

a Parties to armed conflicts, the UN and international bodies should ensure that women have equal participation in the resolution of conflict and in peace processes, as well as in disarmament, demobilization and reintegration programmes.

b Parties to armed conflicts, the UN and other international organizations should ensure the effective collection and destruction of surplus and illegal weapons in the context of peace agreements. To do this effectively women's and other civilian community organizations must be fully involved.

c Civilian and military authorities, and intergovernmental organizations including the UN should ensure that the needs of women and girls are fully incorporated and addressed, in disarmament, demobilization and reintegration programmes.

d The UN and all governments contributing to UN field operations should ensure that their forces do not violate women's human rights. This should include enforcing codes of conduct to protect women from sexual abuse and exploitation, placing women's human rights at the heart of training programmes, and bringing to justice troops that are found to be involved in sexual exploitation and other forms of violence against women.

Chapter 7

Legal background: the international framework

An Afghan family pass a checkpoint during a city-wide weapons crackdown in Kandahar, January 2002.

© AP Photo/John Moore

7: Legal background: the international framework

Under international law, states are obliged to protect women from gender-based violence, including armed violence. They must also take steps to prevent weapons falling into the hands of human rights abusers. This chapter outlines the legal framework that informs and underpins the Stop Violence Against Women and Control Arms campaigns.

International human rights law addresses the rights and dignity of all human beings – women, men and children – at all times and without discrimination. It requires states to respect, protect and fulfil human rights. The most fundamental human rights are "non-derogable", that is, they must be fully respected at all times – even during an emergency such as war. States must prevent, stop, investigate, punish and ensure reparation for violence against women wherever it is likely to occur or has occurred, and whoever the perpetrator.

In times of armed conflict, international humanitarian law (commonly known as the laws of war) offers additional protection, especially to those taking no active part in hostilities. Even in war, the right to use force is not unlimited. International humanitarian law treaties such as the Geneva Conventions protect non-combatants from direct or indiscriminate attacks and other abuse.

General provisions relevant to violence against women

States are obliged to protect women from gender-based violence, including armed violence, under general ("gender-neutral") provisions of international human rights and humanitarian law treaties.

International human rights law:

▶ prohibits gender-based discrimination at all times;[102]

▶ protects the right to life (no one may be arbitrarily deprived of life) at all times;[103]

▶ prohibits torture and other cruel, inhuman or degrading treatment or punishment, including rape and sexual attacks, at all times.[104]

International humanitarian law, which applies in armed conflicts:

▶ prohibits targeting civilians, indiscriminate attacks, and disproportionately or unnecessarily harming civilians when attacking military objectives;[105]

▶ prohibits acts such as torture, rape, outrages on personal dignity (including enforced prostitution and indecent assault), and cruel and humiliating treatment.[106]

Most of these acts are "grave breaches" of the Geneva Conventions and their Additional Protocol I.[107] This means that states which are party to those treaties must either prosecute or extradite suspected perpetrators, whoever they are and wherever the crime took place.

Standards addressing violence against women directly

There are two binding international treaties at the regional level that explicitly address violence against women:

▶ the Inter-American Convention on the Prevention, Punishment and Eradication of Violence Against Women, adopted in 1994;

▶ Protocol to the African Charter on Human and Peoples' Rights on the Rights of Women in Africa, adopted in 2003 (and not as yet in force), which includes extensive provisions prohibiting gender-based violence against women.

The UN Convention on the Elimination of All Forms of Discrimination against Women (CEDAW), an international human rights treaty binding on all states which have joined it, prohibits all forms of discrimination against women. Gender-based violence against women is a form of discrimination, as explained by the Committee on the Elimination of Discrimination against Women, mandated under CEDAW to monitor its implementation, in its General Recommendation No. 19.[108] This recognizes that violence against women impairs women's right to enjoy basic human rights including, the right to life, the right not to be subjected to torture or ill-treatment, the right to equal protection under humanitarian law in times of armed conflict, and the right to liberty and security of the person.[109]

As well as legally binding treaties, there are a number of non-treaty human rights standards which prohibit violence against women. They have been adopted by the UN, regional intergovernmental bodies and other international forums. These include:

▶ the UN Declaration on the Elimination of Violence against Women, adopted in 1993; and

▶ the Beijing Declaration and Platform for Action, adopted in 1995, which set out steps governments should take to protect women from gender-based violence.

'Due diligence' – what states must do to stop violence against women

All states have a duty to protect women from gender-based violence, including armed violence, whether committed by a state official, an abusive husband, a criminal or an armed group. States should exercise "due diligence" to prevent, stop, investigate, punish and ensure reparation for violence against women.

According to Article 4 of the UN Declaration on the Elimination of Violence against Women, "States should pursue by all appropriate means and without delay a policy of eliminating violence against women".

The UN Special Rapporteur on violence against women, its causes and consequences explained the principle of "due diligence" as follows:

"States must promote and protect the human rights of women and exercise due diligence:

a) To prevent, investigate and punish acts of all forms of VAW [violence against women] whether in the home, the workplace, the community or society, in custody or in situations of armed conflict;

b) To take all measures to empower women and strengthen their economic independence and to protect and promote the full enjoyment of all rights and fundamental freedoms;

c) To condemn VAW and not invoke custom, tradition or practices in the name of religion or culture to avoid their obligations to eliminate such violence;

d) To intensify efforts to develop and/or utilize legislative, educational, social and other measures aimed at the prevention of violence, including the dissemination of information, legal literacy campaigns and the training of legal, judicial and health personnel."[110]

General Recommendation No. 19 of the UN Committee on the Elimination of Discrimination against Women states:

"Under general international law and specific human rights covenants, States may also be responsible for private acts if they fail to act with due diligence to prevent violations of rights or to investigate and punish acts of violence, and for providing compensation."[111]

This means that states are responsible for preventing and prosecuting human rights abuses committed by individuals. This is key to combating violence against women, which is often perpetrated by husbands and partners, employers, family members, neighbours, corporations and other individuals ("non-state actors"). For example, it means that states may be held accountable for violence within the family – the most commonly reported type of violence against women – unless they take meaningful steps to prevent or end it.

Law enforcement and the use of force and firearms

Certain police officers are authorized by the state to use force generally, and in particular to hold and use weapons. The UN has adopted standards on how force and weapons may be used while avoiding the violation of basic human rights. The Code of Conduct for Law Enforcement Officials was adopted in 1979 and the Basic Principles on the Use of Force and Firearms by Law Enforcement Officials in 1990.

The core principles require law enforcement officials to:

▶ "as far as possible, apply non-violent means before resorting to the use of force and firearms. They may use force and firearms only if other means remain ineffective or without any promise of achieving the intended result."[112]

▶ use firearms only "when a suspected offender offers armed resistance or otherwise jeopardizes the lives of others and less extreme measures are not sufficient to restrain or apprehend the suspected offender."[113]

If the use of force and firearms is unavoidable, law enforcement officials must, among other things:

"(a) Exercise restraint in such use and act in proportion to the seriousness of the offence and the legitimate objective to be achieved;

(b) Minimize damage and injury, and respect and preserve human life;

(c) Ensure that assistance and medical aid are rendered to any injured or affected persons at the earliest possible moment."[114]

Law enforcement and violence against women

The UN Declaration on the Elimination of Violence against Women calls on all states to "[t]ake measures to ensure that law enforcement officers and public officials responsible for implementing policies to prevent, investigate and punish violence against women receive training to sensitize them to the needs of women".[115]

A Trainer's Guide on Human Rights for the Police, issued by the Office of the UN High Commissioner for Human Rights, recommends, among other things, that police:

▶ ensure that female officers are able to submit complaints and recommendations on gender-related issues of concern to them;

▶ discourage gender-insensitive conversations and jokes; and

▶ review recruitment, hiring, training, and promotion policies to remove any gender bias.[116]

Such institutional practice cannot be effectively organized without recruiting and training women police officers at all levels of command. The UN General Assembly Resolution that adopted the UN Code of Conduct for Law Enforcement Officials states that every law enforcement agency "should be representative of and responsive and accountable to the community as a whole".[117]

Legal obligations in times of war

International humanitarian law applies in situations of armed conflict – not only international wars between states, but also internal armed conflicts between governments and armed groups, or among armed groups. It applies in addition to international human rights law, supplying protections specific to the special circumstances of armed conflict. It lays down standards of conduct for combatants (those taking an active part in hostilities) and their leaders. International humanitarian law treaties protect combatants from certain means and methods of warfare (such as incendiary weapons), but are especially aimed at protecting non-combatants (civilians, medical staff, but also wounded and captured former combatants) from direct or indiscriminate attacks and other abuse. The key legal treaties are the Geneva Conventions (1949) and their Additional Protocols (1977).

Almost all states are parties to the Geneva Conventions and so are legally bound to respect and ensure respect for them. They have a duty to protect non-combatant women and girls and others taking no active part in hostilities from becoming the targets of attack.

The responsibilities of armed groups

Only states can ratify international treaties, but this does not necessarily mean that the international legal rules do not apply to armed groups.

As a matter of customary law (law that is universally established to such an extent that it is binding on all states, whether or not they are bound by treaty law), basic human rights norms apply both to states and to armed groups within states, where they exercise *de facto* control over territory and take on responsibilities analogous to a government. Indeed, in a number of situations armed groups have expressly indicated their commitment to human rights principles. Some innovative approaches have been developed, by UNICEF (the UN Children's Fund) in particular, to elicit commitments from some armed groups to abide by certain human rights norms, such as the UN Convention on the Rights of the Child.

Article 3 common to all four Geneva Conventions applies in all cases of armed conflict and reflects customary international law. Under it, armed groups, no less than governments, must never target civilians, take hostages, or inflict torture or other cruel, inhuman or degrading treatment. More detailed rules for non-international armed conflicts are included in Additional Protocol II to the Geneva Conventions. Some armed groups have taken it upon themselves to respect rules of international humanitarian law. Whether or not an armed group has made a specific commitment, individual members of an armed group can and must be held criminally responsible for war crimes, crimes against humanity, genocide or other serious human rights violations. The adoption of the Rome Statute of the International Criminal Court in 1998 has greatly enhanced the prospects for a world where those who have committed such crimes, whether in the service of governments or of armed groups, will no longer be able to escape justice.

The duty to disobey manifestly illegal orders

All combatants and law enforcement personnel have a duty to refuse to obey manifestly illegal orders. These include orders to commit crimes against humanity, which in turn include, murder, torture, rape, sexual slavery, enforced prostitution, forced pregnancy, enforced sterilization, or any other form of sexual violence of comparable gravity.

The defence that "I was ordered to do it by a superior officer" is not admissible. This principle is enshrined in the Statute of the International Criminal Court, adopted in Rome in 1998. Article 33, entitled "Superior orders and prescription of law", provides:

"1. The fact that a crime within the jurisdiction of the Court has been committed by a person pursuant to an order of a Government or of a superior, whether military or civilian, shall not relieve that person of criminal responsibility unless:

(a) The person was under a legal obligation to obey orders of the Government or the superior in question;

(b) The person did not know that the order was unlawful; and

(c) The order was not manifestly unlawful.

2. For the purposes of this article, orders to commit genocide or crimes against humanity are manifestly unlawful."

International human rights treaties contain similar principles. For instance, the UN Convention against Torture and Other Cruel, Inhuman or Degrading Treatment or Punishment provides: "An order from a superior officer or a public authority may not be invoked as a justification of torture."[118] Similar wording is used in the UN Declaration on the Protection of all Persons from Enforced Disappearance[119] and in the Principles on the Effective Prevention and Investigation of Extra-legal, Arbitrary and Summary Executions.[120]

The control of arms transfers

The UN Programme of Action on Small Arms,[121] agreed in July 2001, requires all participating states to implement a wide range of measures to control small arms and light weapons, including:

▶ safe storage of weapons;

▶ destruction of surpluses;

▶ proper marking and tracing of weapons;

▶ reporting of transfers and control of manufacturing, dealing, brokering and export.

In January 2002, the UN General Assembly called on all states to implement the Programme of Action.[122] In order to prevent arms getting into the wrong hands, participating states committed themselves to: "assess applications for export authorizations according to strict national regulations and procedures that cover all small arms and light weapons and are *consistent with the existing responsibilities of States under relevant international law*" (emphasis added).[123]

But what are these existing responsibilities? The proposed Arms Trade Treaty, inspired by Nobel Peace Laureates, crystallizes these *existing* obligations into a new framework convention (see the main principles in Appendix 1). Support is now building for this document to become an internationally binding treaty, with several governments supporting this initiative, including the governments of Cambodia, Costa Rica, Finland, Kenya, New Zealand, Spain, Tanzania and the UK.

8: The way forward

control arms

Around the world women and men are organizing to tackle armed violence against women, and the wider impact of guns on women's lives. They are campaigning in diverse ways and often in situations of extreme danger. Each of us can play a role in supporting this struggle to end violence against women and to stop the proliferation and misuse of arms.

Everyone must take responsibility. Change must happen at international, national and local levels and must be driven by decision-makers, institutions and individuals alike.

There will only be an end to human rights abuses such as those highlighted in this report when each one of us actively takes our part in ending this violence. When we are silent, or fail to act, we are complicit in the violence, and the threat of violence, that so many women live with every day. It's in our hands to change it!

What can you do about it?

Use this report and the information in it to call for action to address the impact of firearms on women's lives. At the end of chapters 2 to 6 there are brief action points outlining the most important measures that need to be taken to tackle violence against women and the proliferation and misuse of guns in the different contexts of the home and community and during and after conflict. Decide which of these are relevant in your local situation and use them as key campaigning issues. ▶▶▶

▶▶▶ Speak out for women facing armed violence

▶ Demand that your government, international bodies and, where appropriate, armed groups take practical steps to stop armed violence against women.

▶ Condemn armed violence against women whenever and wherever it occurs.

Stop violence against women

▶ Challenge attitudes that foster or reinforce violence against women, and promote gender equality.

▶ Support women who are organizing to stop violence and promote women's equal access to political power, decision-making and resources.

▶ Confront those in authority if they fail to prevent, punish and provide redress for violence against women.

▶ Demand the abolition of national laws that discriminate against women or that allow crimes of violence against women to be committed with impunity.

▶ Insist that your government abides by international human rights agreements.

▶ Visit **www.amnesty.org/actforwomen** to sign up to AI's Stop Violence Against Women Campaign.

Stop arms proliferation and misuse

▶ Campaign for an international Arms Trade Treaty to curb the proliferation of arms leading to violence against women and other human rights abuses.

▶ Demand that national and local authorities enforce strict controls on the possession and use of firearms.

▶ Promote cooperation between government and civil society to make communities safer.

▶ Join the Million Faces petition and encourage others in your community to sign as well. Visit **www.controlarms.org**

Appendix 1: Summary of principles of the proposed Arms Trade Treaty

In October 1995 a group of Nobel Peace Laureates pledged to promote an international initiative to establish an agreement to control the arms trade. Together, they drafted the Nobel Peace Laureates International Code of Conduct on Arms Transfers, which over time has developed into the Arms Trade Treaty. To date, this initiative has been endorsed by 20 individuals and organizations awarded the Nobel Peace Prize.

The proposed Arms Trade Treaty (ATT, also known as the Framework Convention on International Arms Transfers) focuses on commitments of states in respect of the international transfer of arms. It proceeds on the basis that important related issues such as brokering, licensed production, and end-use monitoring will be addressed in subsequent protocols. Those involved in promoting the ATT affirm that the principles and mechanisms it sets out should be applied equally to the broadest possible range of weapons and munitions for use in military operations and law enforcement, including their components, technologies and technical assistance, and material resources for training to make use of such weapons and munitions.

The basic principle of the ATT, set out in **Article 1**, is that all international arms transfers shall be authorized by the appropriate government authority in accordance with its national law. The national law should contain the minimum requirements (to be set out in an annex to the ATT) ensuring that each application for an authorization to transfer arms is reviewed and licensed on an individual basis. The ATT Principles are to be applied as a minimum and shall not prejudice the application of any more stringent national, regional, or international rules, instruments, or requirements.

Articles 2, 3, and 4 of the ATT contain the main obligations of governments when authorizing arms transfers.

Article 2 codifies existing limitations under international law on states' freedom to transfer and to authorize transfers of arms. These limitations include:

- those prohibitions that arise out of the **Charter of the United Nations** (including decisions of the Security Council, such as arms embargoes);

- any **international treaty** to which a state is already bound, including embargoes adopted by other international and regional bodies (such as the European Union) established pursuant to a treaty as well as other agreements containing prohibitions of arms, such as the 1997 Anti-personnel Mines Convention;

- universally accepted principles of **international humanitarian law** including the prohibition on the use of arms that are incapable of distinguishing between combatants and civilians or are of a nature to cause superfluous injury or unnecessary suffering. The prohibition on transfers follows from the appreciation that the transfer of such arms would be irreconcilable with the prohibition under international humanitarian law of the use of such arms. This prohibition would also cover arms the use of which is prohibited by a specific convention but where the convention does not address the question of transfers;

- those arising under or pursuant to **customary international law**. In some circumstances arms transfers from one state to another or to persons in the territory of another state without the latter state's consent will amount to a breach of existing obligations under customary international law relating, for example, to the threat or use of force. Transfers to persons other than those exercising governmental authority may also amount to a breach of the principle of non-intervention in the internal affairs of the state.

Article 3 contains limitations based on the use or likely use of the weapon. This article encompasses the widely accepted principle of international law that a state will not participate in the internationally wrongful acts of another state, as stated in Article 16 of the UN International Law Commission's Articles on Responsibility of States for Internationally Wrongful Acts. Therefore, governments have a responsibility to ensure that the weapons they transfer are not used illegally. The transfer must not proceed if a state knows or ought to know that the arms will be:

- used for breaches of the UN Charter, in particular the prohibition on the threat or use of force in Article 2(4) and related principles concerning threats to peace, breaches of the peace, and acts of aggression in Article 39 of the Charter, in General Assembly Declaration of Principles of International Law of 1970 (General Assembly Resolution 2625 (XXV) of 1970) and in other standard setting UN resolutions;

- used for serious violations of human rights, including violations of the non-derogable provisions of key international conventions such as the 1966 International Covenant on Civil and Political Rights, the 1950 European Convention for the Protection of Human Rights and Fundamental Freedoms, the 1969 American Convention on Human Rights and the 1980 African Charter on Human and Peoples' Rights, and widely accepted multilateral conventions such as the 1984 Convention against Torture and Other Cruel, Inhuman or Degrading Treatment or Punishment;

- used for serious violations of international humanitarian law, including grave breaches of the 1949 Geneva Conventions as well as violations of fundamental principles of international humanitarian law contained in other standard-setting multilateral agreements and in customary international law;

- used in the commission of genocide or crimes against humanity; or

- diverted and used to commit any of the above.

Article 4 does not contain prohibitions on the authorization of arms transfers. Rather, it contains three other factors that governments are required to consider before authorizing an arms transfer. These factors take into account the possible effect of the transfer of arms. Specifically, governments are to consider whether the arms are likely to:

- be used for or to facilitate the commission of violent crimes;

- adversely affect regional security and stability;

- adversely affect sustainable development; or

- be diverted and used to commit any of the above.

Where such circumstances are apparent, the Article establishes a presumption against authorization.

Article 5 of the ATT would require states to establish authorization and licensing mechanisms under their national laws to effectively implement the convention. The legal system of each state would therefore act as the primary enforcement mechanism for the treaty. An Annex (still to be drafted) will develop minimum standards addressing such matters as the need for a transaction-by-transaction licensing mechanism, minimum disclosure requirements by applicants for licences and mechanisms for parliamentary scrutiny.

Article 6 of the ATT would create an International Registry of International Arms Transfers to which contracting parties would be required to submit an annual report on international arms transfers. Although the UN has already established a similar Register of Conventional Arms, it does not include all types of weapons, such as small arms, and is not tied to the implementation of a set of normative standards.

Appendix 2: Guiding principles for work at the community level to reduce gun violence against women

It is impossible to prescribe solutions that would be applicable across the globe for increasing community safety by halting the violence arising from the proliferation and misuse of guns. However, experience does point to some guiding principles.

1   Detailed analysis and understanding of the community and its governance are essential in order to identify the main causes of violence against women in the community and the proliferation and misuse of arms. The research should include all stakeholders, and particularly people who wield power.

2   A holistic view of the situation must be taken, which involves addressing all human rights issues, including civil and political rights (such as the participation of women in public life, police brutality and impunity for offenders) and social, economic and cultural rights (such as access to education, poverty and unemployment). Alternatives to using guns to support livelihoods must be considered.

3   Genuine engagement of the community is imperative. Initiatives must be driven by local people to ensure relevance, participation, shared responsibility and understanding. Political representatives and the police must be representative, accountable and responsive to the community *as a whole*.

4   The needs, perspectives and talents of all members of the community need to be incorporated. This includes men, women, girls, boys, older people, people with disabilities, and people of different ethnicities and religions. For example, former combatants and gang members from different sides may have much in common and can act powerfully for change in challenging gender-based discrimination and violence, and gun culture. Women and women's organizations must be empowered in the face of discrimination to have an equal voice and equal influence in all community initiatives. Ways must be found to provide alternative sources of a sense of identity, purpose, group support, and security for young people, both boys and girls.

5   Partnership between civil society and government is a key factor. Civil society is essential for achieving constructive change, but sustainable change of policy and practice also requires government involvement. Governments can be strong allies, endorsing, strengthening and sustaining the movement for reform, but civil society should be careful to avoid co-option and inducements to legitimize inappropriate government policy. Effective flows of information are critical to ensure effective co-operation.

Endnotes

1. UN Declaration on the Elimination of Violence against Women, UN General Assembly resolution 48/104, 10 December 1993, Article 1.

2. UN Committee on the Elimination of Discrimination against Women, General Recommendation No. 19, Violence against women (Eleventh session, 1992), UN Doc. HRI\GEN\1\Rev.1, para 6.

3. Progress report of Barbara Frey, UN Special Rapporteur on the prevention of human rights violations committed with small arms and light weapons, UN Doc. E/CN.4/Sub.2/2004/37, 21 June 2004, para 50.

4. *Small Arms Survey 2002: Counting the Human Cost*, a project of the Graduate Institute of International Studies Geneva, Oxford University Press, 2002, cited in *Shattered Lives: The case for tough international arms control* (AI Index: ACT 30/001/2003).

5. *It's in our hands: Stop violence against women* (AI Index: ACT 77/001/2004), p.4.

6. World Health Organization, *Small Arms and Global Health*, 2001, cited in the Progress report of Barbara Frey, UN Special Rapporteur on the prevention of human rights violations committed with small arms and light weapons, UN Doc. E/CN.4/Sub.2/2004/37 (2004), www1.umn.edu/humanrts/demo/smallarms2004-2.html.

7. The UN Declaration on the Elimination of Violence against Women gives the following definition of violence against women: "any act of gender-based violence that results in, or is likely to result in, physical, sexual or psychological harm or suffering to women, including threats of such acts, coercion or arbitrary deprivation of liberty, whether occurring in public or in private life." (Article 1)

8. Those involved in promoting the Arms Trade Treaty affirm that the principles and mechanisms laid down in the treaty should be applied equally to the broadest possible range of weapons and munitions for use in military operations and law enforcement, including their components, technologies and technical assistance, and material resources for training to make use of such weapons and munitions.

9. Maryse Jaspard et l'équipe Enveff, "Nommer et compter les violences envers les femmes: une première enquête nationale en France", *POPULATION ET SOCIÉTÉS, bulletin mensuel d'information de l'Institut national d'études démographiques*, Numéro 364, Janvier 2001, www.ined.fr/publications/pop_et_soc/pes364/.

10. *World report on violence and health*, edited by Etienne G. Krug, Linda L. Dahlberg, James A. Mercy, Anthony B. Zwi and Rafael Lozano, World Health Organization, Geneva, 2002.

11. *World report on violence and health*, op cit.

12. Wendy K. Taylor, Lois Magnussen, Mary Jane Amondson, "The Lived Experience of Battered Women", *Violence Against Women*, Vol. 7, No. 5, May 2001.

13. Rachel Jewkes et al, '*He must give me money, he mustn't beat me': Violence against women in three South African provinces*, Medical Research Council, 1999.

14. Zamfara, State of Nigeria, Shari'ah Penal Code Law, January 2000, sec. 76(1) and 76(1)(d) provides that "Nothing is an offence which does not amount to the infliction of grievous hurt upon any person and which is done [*inter alia*]... by a husband for the purpose of correcting his wife." This provision contradicts both Nigeria's Constitution and international treaties to which Nigeria is a state party, including the African Charter on Human and Peoples' Rights, which has been incorporated into Nigeria's domestic law.

15. Patrick Ashby, "Killing Guns in Domestic Abuse: Utilizing protection orders to remove guns from domestic violence", Hart Leadership Program, 2003; available on http://www.pubpol.duke.edu/centers/hlp/programs/sol/overview/research/ashby/interviewtranscripts.html.

16. Henrion Report, Ministry of Health, Paris, February 2001, cited in Ignacio Ramonet, "Violence begins at home", *Le Monde Diplomatique*, July 2004.

17. *"Every six hours a woman is killed by her intimate partner" A National Study of Female Homicide in South Africa*, Gender and Health Research Group, Medical Research Council, Policy Brief No. 5, June 2004.

18. CEMUJER, Clínica de Atención Integral y monitoreo de medios escritos La Prensa Gráfica y El Diario de Hoy, 2002, http://www.isis.cl/temas/vi/dicenque.htm#els.

19. Jacquelyn C. Campbell, Daniel Webster, Jane Koziol-McLain, Carolyn Block, Doris Campbell, Mary Ann Curry, Faye Gary, Nancy Glass, Judith McFarlane, Carolyn Sachs, Phyllis Sharps, Yvonne Ulrich, Susan A. Wilt, Jennifer Manganello, Xiao Xu, Janet Schollenberger, Victoria Frye, and Kathryn Laughon, "Risk Factors for Femicide in Abusive Relationships: Results from a Multisite Case Control Study", *American Journal of Public Health*, July 2003; 93: 1089–1097.

20. D.J. Wiebe, "Homicide and Suicide Risks Associated with Firearms in the Home: A National Case-Control Study", *Annals of Emergency Medicine*, January-June 2003, Volume 41, American College of Emergency Physicians.

21. Henrion Report, op cit. *"Every Six Hours": A National Study of Female Homicide in South Africa*, op cit. FBI, Supplementary Homicide Reports, 1976-2002, cited in Bureau of Justice Statistics, *Homicide trends in the U.S.: Intimate homicide*; page last revised 28 September 2004; available on http://www.ojp.usdoj.gov/bjs/homicide/intimates.htm.

22. "The Lived Experience of Battered Women", op cit.

23. Hemenway D., Shinoda-Tagawa T., Miller M., "Firearm availability and female homicide victimization rates among 25 populous high-income countries", *Journal of the American Medical Women's Association*, 2002 Spring; 57(2):100-4.

24. NSW Bureau of Crime Statistics & Research, Gun and Knife Attacks, Statistical Report No.9, 1973. H Wolfenden, S. Dean, "Gunshot wounds and stabbings: Experience with 124 cases", *Australian & New Zealand Journal of Surgery 57*, 1987, pp19-22. Barlow and Barlow, "More on the role of weapons in homicidal violence", *Med Law 7*, 1988: 347-358. Sarvevaran and Jayewardene, "The role of the weapon in the homicide drama," *Med Law 4*, 1985: 315-326. Peterson et al "Self-inflicted gunshot wounds: Lethality of method versus intent", *Am J Psychiatry* 142(2) February 1985: 228-231.

25. Edna Erez and Shayna Bach, "Immigration, Domestic Violence, and the Military: The Case of 'Military

Brides'", *Violence Against Women*, Vol. 9, No. 9, September 2003.

26 Alex Duval Smith and Bourgoin-Jallieu, "Rugby's brutal world exposed by killing", *The Observer*, London, 15 August 2004.

27 Lisa Vetten, "Reconstruct", *The Sunday Independent*, London, June 2001.

28 Kathleen C. Basile, "Rape by Acquiescence: The Ways in Which Women 'Give in' to Unwanted Sex with Their Husbands", *Violence Against Women*, Vol. 5, No. 9, September 1999.

29 Naeema Abrahams, Dr Rachel Jewkes, "Comments on the Firearms Control Bill Submitted to the Portfolio Safety and Security Committee", 27 January 2000; available on http://www.gca.org.za/bill/submssions/jewkes.htm

30 Letter from Kwing Hung, Canadian Department of Justice, Research and Statistics Division, 25 November 2004.

31 Jenny Mouzos and Catherine Rushforth, "Firearm Related Deaths in Australia, 1991-2001", *Trends and Issues in Crime and Criminal Justice*, No. 269, Australian Institute of Criminology, 2003. www.aic.gov.au/publications/tandi2/tandi269.pdf.

32 "Risk Factors for Femicide in Abusive Relationships: Results From a Multisite Case Control Study", op cit.

33 The Violent Crime Control and Law Enforcement Act of 1994, as amended by the Lautenberg Amendment on Domestic Violence in 1996.

34 Brady Campaign, *Disarming Domestic Violence Abusers: States Should Close Legislative Loopholes That Enable Domestic Abusers to Purchase and Possess Firearms*, September 2003, http://endabuse.org/programs/ publicpolicy/files/BradyReport.pdf.

35 "Closing Illegal Gun Markets: Extending Criminal Background Checks to All Gun Sales", Educational Fund to Stop Violence, May 2002.

36 *"I don't want to die", Domestic violence in Iraq* (AI Index: MDE 14/001/2004).

37 Penny Parenzee, Lillian Artz and Kelley Moult, *Monitoring the Implementation of the Domestic Violence Act: First Research Report 2000-2001*, Consortium on Violence Against Women, published by the Institute of Criminology, University of Cape Town, 2001, pp. 64-65.

38 G. Satherley, T. Hewett, H. Signy, "Gunman slaughters six – Family feud on Central Coast", *Sydney Morning Herald*, 28 October 1992.

39 United Nations, International Study on Firearm Regulation, August 1999 update, Belarus, cited on SAFER-Net, http://www.research.ryerson.ca/SAFER-Net/regions/Europe/Blr_JL03.

40 See, for example, the Firearms Act 1996 (New South Wales), Firearms Act 1996 (Victoria), Firearms Act 1977 (South Australia) (as amended in 1996). In 1996 and 1997 all the states and territories of Australia amended their gun laws to comply with the National Firearms Agreement adopted in May 1996.

41 Ozanne-Smith J., Ashby K., Newstead S., Stathakis V.Z. and Clapperton, A., "Firearm related deaths: the impact of regulatory reform", *Injury Prevention*, 2004, 10:280-286.

42 http://www.mothersagainstguns.org

43 Adele Kirsten, "Women Making the Links: Women, Peace and Justice", keynote address at "In the Line of Fire: A Gender Perspective on Small Arms Proliferation, Peace Building and Conflict Resolution", Palais des Nations, Geneva, 7-8 March 2001.

44 For a global review and elaboration of policing firearms standards, see *Guns and Policing: Standards to Prevent Misuse* (AI Index: ACT 30/001/2004) and Brian Wood with Glenn MacDonald, "Critical Triggers: implementing international standards for police firearms use", *Small Arms Survey 2004: Rights at Risk*, www.smallarmssurvey.org.

45 Amnesty International, *The Wire*, September 2004.

46 See *Guns and Policing: Standards to Prevent Misuse* and "Critical Triggers: implementing international standards for police firearms use", op cit.

47 Mumbi Risah, "Raped by a Gun", *The Devastating Impact of Small Arms and Light Weapons on the Lives of Women*, IANSA Women's Caucus, 2001.

48 *Solomon Islands: Women confronting violence* (AI Index: 43/001/2004).

49 See, for example, *Nigeria: Repression of women's protests in oil-producing delta region* (AI Index: AFR 44/008/2003).

50 "The Lived Experience of Battered Women", *Violence Against Women*, op cit.

51 *Afghanistan: "No one listens to us and no one treats us as human beings"– Justice denied to women* (AI Index: ASA 11/023/2003).

52 *Monitoring the Implementation of the Domestic Violence Act: First Research Report 2000-2001*, op cit, p.104.

53 "Killing Guns in Domestic Abuse: Utilizing protection orders to remove guns from domestic violence", op cit.

54 "Finding True Peace in Post-War Bosnia-Herzegovina", UNIFEM Trustfund, Telling the Stories, available on http://www.unifem.org/index.php?f_page_pid=168.

55 David Fickling, "Raskol gangs rule world's worst city", *The Guardian*, London, 22 September 2004.

56 See *Small Arms Survey 2004: Rights at Risk*, op cit, www.smallarmssurvey.org.

57 Patrick Ashby, "Killing Guns in Domestic Abuse: Utilizing protection orders to remove guns from domestic violence", op cit.

58 David Fickling, "Raskol gangs rule world's worst city", *The Guardian*, London, 22 September 2004.

59 Brian Wood, Undule Mwakasungura and Robert Phiri, *Malawi Security Sector Reform: Pilot Project Report*, Lilongwe, August 2000.

60 *Malawi Security Sector Reform: Pilot Project Report*, op cit.

61 Undule Mwakasungura, *Armed Violence in Malawi: An analysis of Press Reports*, 26 June 2000.

62 Testimony by women to Malawi Community Policing Forums, 2000 and 2001.

63 Human Rights Watch, *Climate of Fear: Sexual Violence and Abduction of Women and Girls in Baghdad*, July 2003.

64 *Viva Rio*, Brazil, cited in *Shattered Lives: the case for tough international arms control*, op cit.

65 "Gun crime: Has anything changed?", *BBC News Online*, 29 April 2004.

66 See *Small Arms Survey 2004: Rights at Risk*, op cit, chapter 2.

67 "Criminals fund gun crime fight", *BBC News Online*, 19 July 2003.

68 Patrick Luganda, "Grace Loumo Spearheads The Karamoja Women's Peace Drive," The New Vision, 14 October 2003, cited in Christina M. Yeung, *Gender Perspectives on Small Arms Proliferation in Karamoja*, United Nations University, forthcoming publication.

69 Taken from *Viva Rio* interviews with focus group of girls and young women, aged 14-23, January 2004.

70 Rebecca Allison, "Anniversary of the Aston murders brings little progress in reclaiming the streets," *The Guardian*, London, 1 January 2004.

71 Article 5 of Convention on the Elimination of All Forms of Discrimination against Women specifically calls on states to "modify the social and cultural patterns of conduct of men and women, with a view to achieving the elimination of prejudices and customary and all other practices which are based on the idea of the inferiority or the superiority of either of the sexes or on stereotyped roles for men and women."

72 UN Security Council Resolution 1325, www.un.org/events/res_1325e.pdf.

73 *Sierra Leone: Rape and other forms of sexual violence against girls and women* (AI Index: AFR 51/035/2000).

74 Amnesty International – *Universal Children's Day Action: Israel and the Occupied Territories and the Palestinian Authority – Act Now to Stop the Killing of Children!* (AI Index: MDE 02/002/2004).

75 *Universal Children's Day Action: Israel and the Occupied Territories and the Palestinian Authority – Act Now to Stop the Killing of Children!*, op cit.

76 See *Shattered Lives: The case for tough international arms controls*, op cit.

77 *Democratic Republic of Congo; Mass rape – time for remedies* (AI Index: AFR 62/018/2004).

78 *Democratic Republic of Congo; Mass rape – time for remedies*, op cit.

79 Vanessa Farr, "Men, women and guns: Understanding how gender ideologies support small arms and light weapons proliferation." Bonn International Center for Conversion (BICC), *Conversion Survey 2003: Global Disarmament, Demilitarization and Demobilization*. Nomos Verlagsgesellschaft: Baden-Baden Germany, 2003: 120-133.

80 Liz Philipson, *Conflict in Nepal: Perspectives on the Maoist Movement*, Centre for the Study of Global Governance, London School of Economics and Political Science, May 2002.

81 See Coalition to Stop the Use of Child Soldiers, *Child Soldiers: Global Report 2004*.

82 *Liberia: The promises of peace for 21,000 child soldiers*, 17 May 2004 (AI Index: AFR 34/006/2004).

83 Human Rights Watch, *Bosnia and Hercegovina: "A Closed Dark Place": Past and Present Human Rights Abuses in Foca*, July 1998, www.hrw.org/reports98/foca. See also *Prosecutor v. Kunarac et al*, ICTY Case No. IT-96-23 and IT-96-23/1, Trial Chamber II, Judgment of 22 February 2001.

84 *Bosnia and Hercegovina: "A Closed Dark Place": Past and Present Human Rights Abuses in Foca*, op cit. See also *Prosecutor v. Kunarac et al*, ICTY Case No. IT-96-23 and IT-96-23/1, Trial Chamber II, Judgment of 22 February 2001.

85 http://www.womenwarpeace.org/solomon_islands/ solomon_islands.htm

86 "Women who brought peace to the Solomon Islands", Caritas Australia News Room, available on http://www.caritas.org.au/newsroom/news_from_field_si. htm

87 *Ending Violence Against Women: A Challenge for Development and Humanitarian Work*, Francine Pickup with Suzanne Williams and Caroline Sweetman, Oxford, Oxfam GB, 2001, cited in *Shattered Lives: The case for tough international arms controls*, op cit.

88 Zorica Mrsevic and Donna M. Hughes, "Violence Against Women in Belgrade, Serbia: SOS Hotline 1990-1993", *Violence Against Women*, Vol. 3, No. 2, 1997.

89 World Health Organization (WHO), Geneva, 2002, *World Report on Violence and Health*, p.15.

90 *Afghanistan: "No one listens to us and no one treats us as human beings" – Justice denied to women*, op cit.

91 *Take the Guns Away: Afghan Voices on Security and Elections*, op cit.

92 The Human Rights Research and Advocacy Consortium (HRRAC), *Take the Guns Away: Afghan Voices on Security and Elections*, Kabul, September 2004.

93 According to UN Secretary-General Kofi Annan, "In order to be successful, DDR [disarmament, demobilization and reintegration] initiatives must be based on a concrete understanding of who combatants are – women, men, girls, boys. Recent analyses of DDR processes from a gender perspective have highlighted that women combatants are often invisible and their needs are overlooked." The Secretary-General's Study. Women Peace and Security. UN, New York. 2002, cited in UNIFEM, *Getting it Right, Doing it Right: Gender and Disarmament, Demobilization and Reintegration*, October 2004, New York, http://www.womenwarpeace.org/issues/ddr/ gettingitright.pdf.

94 Mazurana, D., McKay, S., Carlson, K., Kasper, J., "Girls in fighting forces and groups: Their recruitment, participation, demobilization and reintegration," in *Peace and Conflict, Journal of Peace Psychology*, 8, 2, pp. 97-123, copyright Lawrence Erlbaum Associates Inc.

95 *Precious resources – Adolescents in the Reconstruction of Sierra Leone*, Women's Commission for Refugee Women and Children, September 2002.

96 See *Liberia: One year after Accra – immense human rights challenges remain* (AI Index: AFR 34/012/2004).

97 The Comprehensive Peace Agreement was signed in Accra, Ghana, on 18 August 2003. On 19 September 2003 the UN Security Council decided to deploy a large peacekeeping operation, the UN Mission in Liberia (UNMIL).

98 "Fourth progress report of the Secretary-General on the United Nations Mission in Liberia," 10 September 2004, UN document S/2004/725, and UN Security Council Resolution 1561 (2004), 17 September 2004, UN Doc. S/RES/1561. The international community made generous pledges at the International Reconstruction Conference in New York in February 2004, but by September 2004 only half of those pledges have been redeemed.

99 *Despite promises violence against women continues unabated* (AI Index: ACT 77/078/2004).

100 Statement by the President of the Security Council, adopted by the Security Council on 28 October 2004.

101 *Getting it Right, Doing it Right: Gender and Disarmament, Demobilization and Reintegration,* op cit.

102 See, for instance, in Articles 2(1), 3, 4(1), 23(4), 24 and 26 of the International Covenant on Civil and Political Rights (ICCPR, 1966); UN Convention on the Elimination of All Forms of Discrimination against Women (CEDAW, 1979).

103 See, for instance, Articles 6(1) and 4(2) of the ICCPR.

104 See, for instance, Articles 7 and 4(2) of the ICCPR, Articles 1, 2 and 16 of the UN Convention against Torture and Other Cruel, Inhuman or Degrading Treatment or Punishment (1984).

105 See, for instance, Articles 48-58 of the Protocol Additional to the Geneva Conventions of 12 August 1949, and relating to the Protection of Victims of International Armed Conflicts (Additional Protocol I, 1977).

106 See, for instance, Article 3(1) common to all four Geneva Conventions; Article 17 of Geneva Convention III relative to the Treatment of Prisoners of War (1949), Articles 5, 27, 32, 37 of Geneva Convention IV relative to the Protection of Civilian Persons in Time of War (1949); Articles 75(2)(a)(ii); 75(2)(b); 75(2)(e) of Additional Protocol I, Articles 4(2)(a), 4(2)(e), 4(2)(h) of Protocol II Additional to the Geneva Conventions of 12 August 1949 and relating to the Protection of Victims of Non-International Armed Conflicts (Additional Protocol II, 1977).

107 See, for instance, Article 130 of the 3rd Geneva Convention; Article 147 of the 4th Geneva Convention; Articles 11, 85 of Additional Protocol I.

108 Committees charged with monitoring the implementation of a UN human rights treaties occasionally produce general recommendations or general comments. These provide guidance to states parties both as to the meaning of specific provisions of the treaty and as to what states should include in their reports to the committee on steps they take to ensure its implementation.

109 Committee on the Elimination of Discrimination against Women, General Recommendation No. 19, Violence against women, UN Doc. A/47/38, 29 January 1992.

110 Radhika Coomaraswamy, Special Rapporteur on violence against women, Report to the Commission on Human Rights, UN Doc. E/CN.4/2003/75, 6 January 2003, para 85.

111 Committee on the Elimination of Discrimination against Women, General Recommendation No. 19, Violence against women, (Eleventh session, 1992), Compilation of General Comments and General Recommendations Adopted by Human Rights Treaty Bodies, U.N. Doc. HRI\GEN\1\Rev.1 at 84 (1994), para 9.

112 Principle 4 of the Basic Principles on the Use of Force and Firearms by Law Enforcement Officials (UN Basic Principles), adopted by the Eighth United Nations Congress on the Prevention of Crime and the Treatment of Offenders, Havana, Cuba, 27 August to 7 September 1990.

113 Code of Conduct for Law Enforcement Officials, adopted by UN General Assembly resolution 34/169 of 17 December 1979, Article 3, Commentary.

114 Principle 5 of the UN Basic Principles on the Use of Force and Firearms by Law Enforcement Officials.

115 Article 4(i).

116 Office of the United Nations High Commissioner for Human Rights, Human Rights and Law Enforcement, *A Trainer's Guide on Human Rights for the Police.* United Nations. Professional Training Series No.5/Add.2. New York and Geneva, 2002, pp. 223-224; www.unhchr.ch/html/menu6/2/train5add2.pdf.

117 General Assembly resolution 34/169 of 17 December 1979, preamble, paragraph (a), which is referred to as an "additional important principle and prerequisite for the humane performance of law enforcement functions".

118 Article 2(3) of the UN Convention against Torture and Other Cruel, Inhuman or Degrading Treatment or Punishment (1984).

119 General Assembly Resolution 47/133 of 18 December 1992.

120 Recommended by UN Economic and Social Council resolution 1989/65 of 24 May 1989.

121 UN Programme of Action to Prevent, Combat and Eradicate the Illicit Trade in Small Arms and Light Weapons in All Its Aspects.

122 UNGA resolution 56/24; 10 January 2002.

123 UN Programme of Action to Prevent, Combat and Eradicate the Illicit Trade in Small Arms and Light Weapons in All Its Aspects, Part II, para 11.

124 *Small Arms Survey 2004: Rights at Risk,* op cit.

125 *Small Arms Survey 2002: Counting the Human Cost,* cited in *Shattered Lives: The case for tough international arms control,* op cit.

Violence Against Women
– global human rights scandal

**STOP
VIOLENCE
AGAINST
WOMEN**

AMNESTY
INTERNATIONAL

Violence against women is one of the greatest human rights scandals of our times. From birth to death, in times of peace as well as war, women face discrimination and violence at the hands of the state, the community and the family. Violence against women is not confined to any particular political or economic system, but is prevalent in every society in the world and cuts across boundaries of wealth, race and culture. The power structures within society which perpetuate violence against women are deep-rooted and intransigent. The experience or threat of violence inhibits women everywhere from fully exercising and enjoying their human rights.

Women throughout the world have organized to expose and counter violence against women and discrimination. They have achieved dramatic changes in the landscape of laws, policies and practices. They have brought the violations, which are characteristically hidden from scrutiny, into the public arena. They have established that violence against women demands a response from governments, communities and individuals. Above all, they have challenged the view of women as passive victims of violence. Even in the face of hardship, poverty and repression, women are leading the struggle to fight discrimination and violence against women.

Change must come at international, national and local levels. It must be brought about by governments as well as private actors, by institutions as well as individuals. International treaties must be respected, laws must be adopted or abolished, support systems must be put in place and above all attitudes, prejudices and social beliefs that foster and reinforce violence against women must change.

Preventing violence against women requires us to:

▶ Speak out against violence against women, listen to women and believe them;

▶ Condemn violence against women as a major human rights scandal;

▶ Confront those in authority if they fail to prevent, punish and redress violence against women;

▶ Challenge religious, social, and cultural attitudes and stereotypes which diminish women's humanity;

▶ Promote women's equal access to political power, decision-making and resources; and

▶ Support women to organize themselves to stop the violence.